The Little
Big Book
of
Christmas

The Little Big Book of Christmas

Edited by
Lena Tabori

Designed by
Timothy Shaner

A Welcome Book

William Morrow
and Company, Inc.

NEW YORK

Copyright © 1999 by Welcome Enterprises, Inc.

Additional copyright information on page 352.

Produced by Welcome Enterprises, Inc.
588 Broadway, New York, N.Y. 10012

Project Director: Alice Wong
Editorial Assistants: Natasha Tabori Fried and Elizabeth Kessler

Library of Congress Cataloging-in-Publication Data
The little big book of Christmas / edited by Lena Tabori ; designed by
    Timothy Shaner. -- 1st ed.
        p.   cm.
    "A Welcome book."
    ISBN 0-688-17414-0
    1. Christmas. 2. Christmas stories. 3. Christmas cookery.
    I. Tabori, Lena.
    GT4985.L57   1999
    394.2663--dc21   99-30364
                                              CIP

Printed in Singapore

FIRST EDITION
1 2 3 4 5 6 7 8 9 10

www.williammorrow.com

CONTENTS

CAROLS

POEMS

CONTENTS

CONTENTS

RECIPES

FOREWORD

My Christmases have done a lot of evolving over the years. When I was very little growing up in Sweden, they were a formal affair. Only the immediate family attended, food was served on silver, the tree was filled with real burning candles, and my grandmother made hard caramel candies in little paper cups. When I was three years old we moved to Los Angeles, and my mother tried to recreate Sweden in our home. But I knew we were in America when the actor, Audie Murphy, dressed up as Santa and walked up our driveway through a cluster of orange and grapefruit groves. We welcomed him with warm saffron bread.

These days, Christmas is still filled with candles and dinner is still served on my grandmother's china. My mother arranged the Nativity for my children as she had done for me and my brothers, and now my eldest daughter, Natasha, continues the tradition. Traditional Swedish favorites like gingerbread cookies, and meatballs with lingonberries still dominate the menu. And children are still central. It takes us all (kids and grownups!) almost two days to bake the cookies—days during which Christmas carols and the smell of simmering glögg fill the house.

FOREWORD

But now, friends join family for an ever-larger Christmas Eve celebration. Tiny colored lights illuminate the tree, and we have added a gift grab-bag. Each of our guests brings an inexpensive (but creatively chosen) present, and these are the gifts we unwrap and fight over (amidst laughter) before dessert. On Christmas morning, we do stockings.

Through my younger daughter Katrina's marriage to Matty, we have also discovered the ritual of caroling. Every year at her in-laws we join their family and friends to sing. This is a simple, loving evening, as much about music as it is about Christmas. And what beautiful music it is.

Holidays grow and change as we do. My daughters' Christmases are not the same as mine were, and my grandchildren's will doubtless be different still. But as we add and subtract traditions, I doubt we will ever lose the heart of Christmas. This collection of stories, carols, poems, and recipes speaks from and to that heart. From the quiet and awe we feel listening to St. Matthew, to the tears we shed reading *The Birds' Christmas Carol*, or the laughter we share decorating our brilliant (or not so brilliant) cookies, this book is about being together, about peace and love, and about joy. These are the rituals my family carries and protectively passes down from generation to generation.

—From my family to yours, Lena Tabori

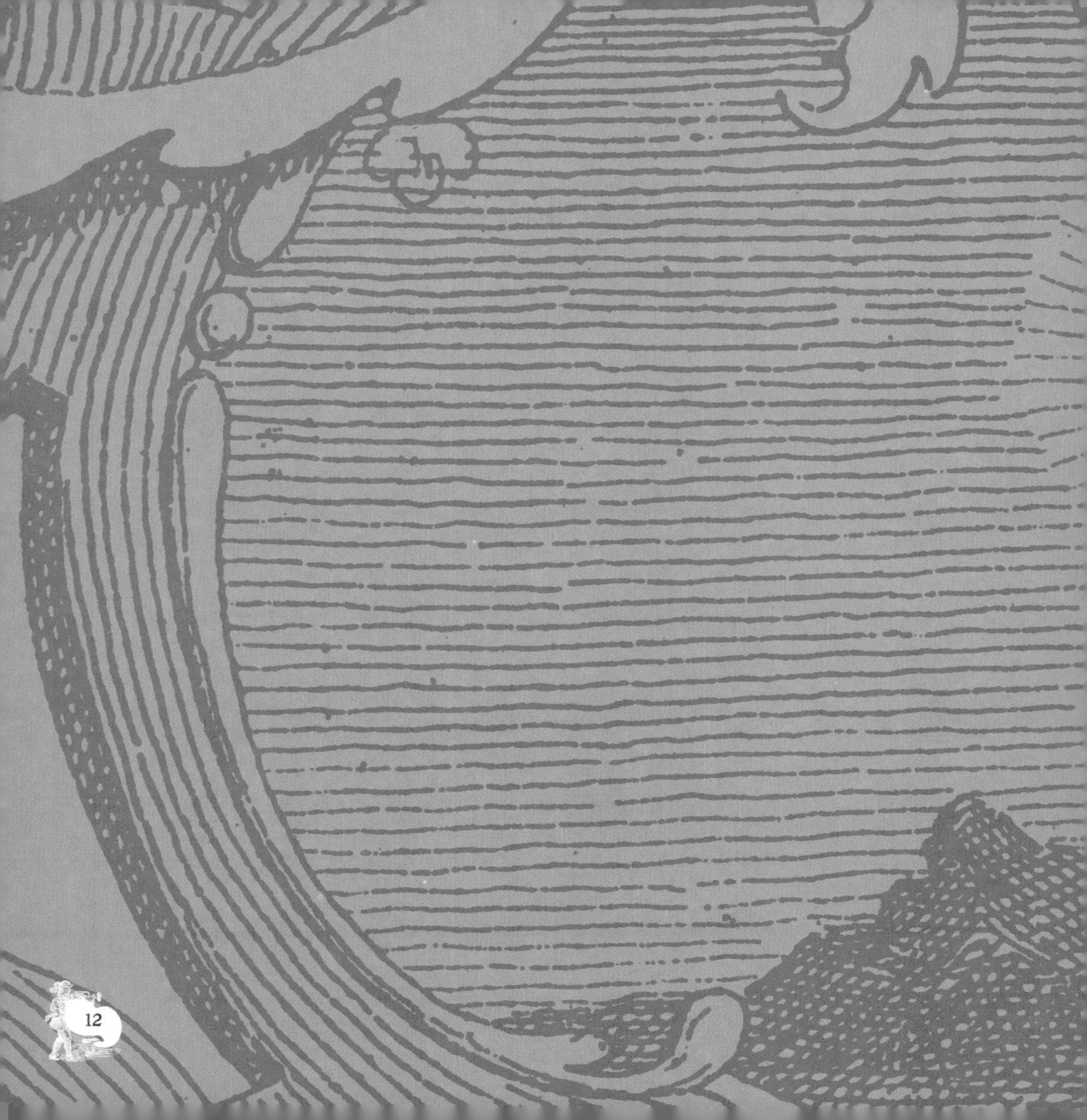

Some say...

William Shakespeare

Some say that ever 'gainst that season comes
Wherein our Saviour's birth is celebrated,
The bird of dawning singeth all night long:
And then, they say, no spirit dare stir abroad,
The nights are wholesome, then no planets strike,
No fairy takes nor witch hath power to charm,
So hallow'd and so gracious is the time.

—*Hamlet*, Act 1, Scene 1

Born in Bethlehem

(St. Luke 2:1-16)

And it came to pass in those days, that there went out a decree from Caesar Augustus, that all the world should be taxed.

(*And* this taxing was first made when Cyrenius was governor of Syria.)

And all went to be taxed, every one into his own city.

And Joseph also went up from Galilee, out of the city of Nazareth, into Judæa, unto the city of David, which is called Bethlehem; (because he was of the house and lineage of David:)

To be taxed with Mary his espoused wife, being great with child.

And so it was, that, while they were there, the days were accomplished that she should be delivered.

And she brought forth her firstborn son, and wrapped him in swaddling clothes, and laid him in a manger; because there was no room for them in the inn.

And there were in the same country shepherds abiding in the field, keeping watch over their flock by night.

And, lo, the angel of the Lord

16

came upon them, and the glory of the Lord shone round about them: and they were sore afraid.

And the angel said unto them, Fear not: for, behold, I bring you good tidings of great joy, which shall be to all people.

For unto you is born this day in the city of David a Saviour, which is Christ the Lord.

And this *shall* be a sign unto you; Ye shall find the babe wrapped in swaddling clothes, lying in a manger.

And suddenly there was with the angel a multitude of the heavenly host praising God, and saying,

Glory to god in the highest, and on earth peace, good will toward men.

And it came to pass, as the angels were gone away from them into heaven, the shepherds said one to another, Let us now go even unto Bethlehem, and see this thing which is come to pass, which the Lord hath made known unto us.

And they came with haste, and found Mary, and Joseph, and the babe lying in a manger.

❋

The Three Wise Men

(St. Matthew 2:1-14)

Now when Jesus was born in Bethlehem of Judæa in the days of Herod the king, behold, there came wise men from the east to Jerusalem.

Saying, Where is he that is born King of the Jews? for we have seen his star in the east, and are come to worship him.

When Herod the king had heard *these things*, he was troubled, and all Jerusalem with him.

And when he had gathered all the chief priests and scribes of the people together, he demanded of them where Christ should be born.

And they said unto him, In Bethlehem of Judæa: for thus it is written by the prophet,

And thou Bethlehem, *in* the land of Juda, art not the least among the princes of Juda: for out of thee shall come a Governor, that shall rule my people Israel.

Then Herod, when he had

privily called the wise men, enquired of them diligently what time the star appeared.

And he sent them to Bethlehem, and said, Go and search diligently for the young child; and when ye have found *him*, bring me word again, that I may come and worship him also.

When they had heard the king, they departed; and, lo, the star, which they saw in the east, went before them, till it came and stood over where the young child was.

When they saw the star, they rejoiced with exceeding great joy.

And when they were come into the house, they saw the young child with Mary his mother, and fell down, and worshipped him: and when they had opened their treasures, they presented unto him gifts; gold, and frankincense, and myrrh.

And being warned of God in a dream that they should not return to Herod, they departed into their own country another way.

And when they were departed, behold, the angel of the Lord appeareth to Joseph in a dream, saying, Arise, and take the young child and his mother, and flee into Egypt, and be thou there until I bring thee word: for Herod will seek the young child to destroy him.

When he arose, he took the young child and his mother by night, and departed into Egypt.

❄

The First Noel

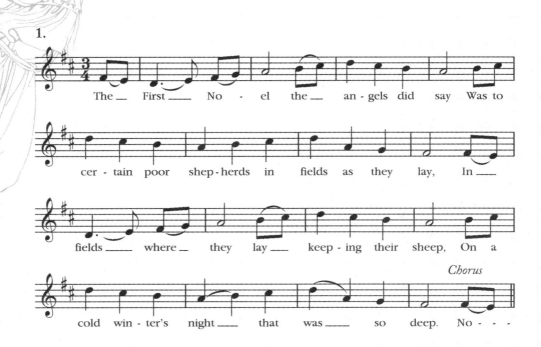

1.

The __ First __ No - el the __ an - gels did say Was to
cer - tain poor shep - herds in fields as they lay, In __
fields __ where __ they lay __ keep - ing their sheep, On a
cold win - ter's night __ that was __ so deep. No - - -

Chorus

el, _____ No - - - el, No - - - el, No - el,

Born is the King _____ of Is - - - ra - el.

2. They looked up and saw a star
   Shining in the East beyond them far,
   And to the earth it gave great light,
   And so it continued both day
       and night.

   Chorus

3. This star drew nigh to the
       Northwest,
   O'er Bethlehem it took its rest,
   And there it did both stop and stay,
   Right over the place where Jesus lay.

Chorus

4. Then entered in those wisemen three,
   Full rev'rently upon their knee,
   And offered there in His presence,
   Their gold and myrrh and
       frankincense.

Chorus

23

The Three Magi

Pura Belpré

Llegan de noche con gran cantela
Cuando ninguno sus pasos vela
Y al dormitoria del niño van
Y al dormitoria del niño van.

Swiftly they come in the night
As every one sleeps
And no one their footsteps watches
Then to the children's bedroom they go
Then to the children's bedroom they go.

It was the fifth of January, the eve of the "Three Kings" day. The day when all Spanish children eagerly await their Christmas presents.

In the sumptuous Palace of the Orient, where the Magi Kings lived, reigned great excitement and confusion. The Royal doorman had been busy all morning answering the bell as the couriers came from the four corners of the world, bringing the royal mail. Inside the palace, the Champerlain's voice could be heard giving orders to his hundred servants.

"Open the windows," he shouted, and a hundred men glittering in uniforms decked with gold and silver, in which the initials "M.M." (Magi Messengers) stood out, ran from one side of the spacious hall to the other, and opened wide the royal windows, letting in the cool air.

Kerchoo! Kerchoo! sneezed the Chamberlain.

"Bring my highest powdered wig," he called.

Again the hundred servants darted on, getting in each other's way, stumbling over chairs and sofas, until finally a very tall and thin one was able to free himself from the rest and bring out an immense wig, which he placed on the Chamberlain's head.

In the Royal kitchen the noise rose like a thunderous wave. Like a captain before his army, and clad in white apron and high cap, the royal chef stood. With hands folded across his voluminous stomach, he gravely directed his men. They carried out his orders with dexterity and care.

At his signal eggs were broken and beaten to soft fluffy foam, flour kneaded and almonds and nuts grated to a fine powder. From the oven and frying pans rose the smell of sweetmeats and roasts. It was evident that in the Royal Kitchen of the Three Magi, the innumerable cooks were getting ready an immense repast for a long journey.

Outside the palace in the Royal stables, the stamping and neighing of the Royal horses could be heard for miles around. Lines and lines of coaches, covered with heavy blankets, could be seen down the hall.

"There comes Carlos again," whispered a dapple grey horse to another.

"Stop your stamping, stop it this minute," called out Carlos as he opened the door.

In reply the horses raised their heads and neighed loudly.

"I know, I know," said Carlos, "but this is the eve of the "Three Kings' day, and it's the camels the Magi want and not horses."

Slowly he opened the door and led the camels to the public square. Already people were gathered there, while the stable hands brought gallons of water, baskets of scented soaps and a great number of combs and brushes.

The Royal Camels were about to receive their bath and this was a ceremony always performed in public. First the water was poured reverently over their backs. Then the stable boys divided in groups of ten and armed with soap and brushes began the scrubbing. This finished, another group would begin the combing and smoothing of the hair. Decked then with red mantles and silver reins, the three choice stable boys Carlos, Juan and Pedro led them to the door of the Royal Palace. The three magnificent looking camels of the Three Magi were the happiest camels in the entire world, for it was the 5th of January and they were to carry on their backs the three most-wished-for persons in the children's world—King Gaspar, King Melchor, and King Baltazar. But they were impatient as they stood there. Putting their three heads together they asked each other:

"Where are the Three Magi? Why do they keep us waiting?"

And well might they ask, for the Three Kings could hardly be seen at that time.

In the Grand Throne Room, behind a barricade of opened envelopes they sat laughing and nodding to each other, as they read and carefully put away millions of letters sent to them.

There were letters of all sizes and colors. Some of them were written on fine paper with gilt borders, others embellished with flowers and birds, written in clear and legible handwriting, but the majority of them, and these were the ones the Kings liked best, were written on scraps of paper, and full of dots of ink and many erasures. They all carried the same message—a plea for some particular toy and a promise to be a better boy or girl in the future.

At last, the last letter was read and carefully put away. Slowly the Three Magi rose from their beautiful thrones and left the room. The Royal doorman saw them coming and opened the door wide. Solemn in their approach, majestic in their bearing, handsomely garbed with precious stones and jewelry, and with their ermine coats about them, the Three Magi of the Orient appeared at the door ready to mount their camels.

"How beautiful and handsome they are," said Carlos to the other stable boys as they held the camels for the Magi to mount.

Large parcels of food and pastries, jugs of water and innumerable baskets full of all kinds of toys were brought out and tied tightly on the camels' backs.

They were soon off while the servants waved and wished them good luck.

On and on they went.

As they entered the desert, night fell.

"Dark and somber indeed is the night," said King Gaspar.

"Fear not," remarked King Melchor, "the star will soon appear to guide us, as it appears every year. The same star that led us twenty centuries ago to the stable at Bethlehem."

He had hardly finished talking when up above their heads appeared a strange star glittering in the dark.

"Here is the star," said King

Melchor again.

"Seems to me," said King Baltazar, "that on our last journey the star always appeared much later; however I may have lost all sense of time."

They followed the course it led . . . On and on they went.

For hours they travelled.

Suddenly from behind a cloud a ray of light appeared and darkness gave way to daylight.

The sun came out and the strange star disappeared.

Slowly the Three Magi pulled up their reins.

"Alas," they exclaimed. "What is the meaning of this?"

To their great surprise after having ridden away in the night, they were standing at their very door—the door of their own castle.

"What can this mean?" said King Gaspar.

"It means," answered King Melchor, "that in the course of the evening we have come back to our starting point."

"But we followed the star," said King Baltazar in a doleful voice.

"That was no star," piped a small voice.

"Wh-who speaks?" called out King Baltazar—this time in an excited voice.

"Oh, only me," said a little black beetle coming out from one of the camel's ears.

30

"You!" cried King Melchor, "how do you know?" "Tell us, little black beetle, tell us all you know," said King Gaspar.

"The star," said the little beetle, trying to raise its voice loud enough for them to hear, "was just a number of fireflies in formation to imitate a star."

"What are we to do?" moaned King Melchor. "We will never reach Spain. For the first time the children will find their shoes empty. What are we to do?"

"Shush—" said the beetle. "Look!"

Towards them running so fast his thin legs scarcely touched the ground, was coming a little grey mouse.

"Raton Perez!" exclaimed the Kings.

Making a low bow, he said:

"Yes, Raton Perez—bearer of good news!"

"Speak then," said the Kings.

"My Kings," said Raton Perez, "it's all the fault of the horses. They are very jealous. While they discussed their plans with the fireflies, I chanced to be resting on a bundle of straw. Too late to follow you, I thought of a plan to undo the fireflies' work. What could be easier than to ask Father Time? It was as you know a question of time and only He could arrange it. To my great surprise, I found Father Time sound asleep over his great cloak. Not to cause him the least discomfort, lest I should awaken him, I set his clock twenty-four hours back. So now my good Magi, ride on! The children of Spain must have their toys."

As if led by an invisible hand, the three camels pricked up their ears, raised their heads and went on towards the desert. Silence

31

descended upon the group again. Above them the blue sky and all around them the sand, hot like fire under the rays of the sun. The Magi looked at each other in silence and set their eyes on the road.

Darkness soon closed in. On and on the camels went. They could hardly see themselves in the darkness that enveloped them.

Suddenly a star appeared large and resplendent, way up in the sky. Its light shone like a silver thread on the sand. In great silence, the Three Magi raised their heads to the sky, and gazed long at the star. There was hope and faith in the three eager faces that now bent their heads to lead the camels on.

From somewhere a sound of bells was heard, faintly at first, then louder and louder.

"God be praised," said King Baltazar, "we are near the city. It's the tolling of the bells—the bells from the church tower, ringing as a reminder of the entrance at Bethlehem years ago, letting us know, as they always do, that we are close to the city gates.

Ding—Dong—Ding—Dong—

The bells chimed merrily now and the hour of twelve struck. The camels shook their heads making all their headgear tinkle. Strangely enough they picked up the tempo of the bells and almost in unison passed the opened gate into the city.

That morning under each bed, inside each shoe, beside baskets and boxes wrapped with straw and flowers the children found their gifts, unaware of the hardships the Three Magi had in keeping faith with them.

❄

We Three Kings of Orient Are

1.

We Three Kings of O - ri - ent Are,

bear - ing gifts we tra - verse a - far.

Field and foun - tain, moor and moun - tain,

Refrain

fol - low - ing yon - der star. O, _____

star of wan - der, star of night!

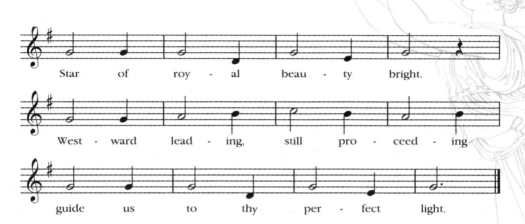

Star of roy - al beau - ty bright.

West - ward lead - ing, still pro - ceed - ing

guide us to thy per - fect light.

2. Born a King on Bethlehem plain,
   Gold I bring to crown Him again,
   King forever, Ceasing never
   Over us all to reign.

   Refrain

3. Frankincense to offer have I,
   Incense owns a Deity night:
   Prayer and praising, All men raising,
   Worship Him, God on high.

   Refrain

4. Myrrh is mine; its bitter perfume
   Breathes a life of gathering gloom;
   Sorrowing, sighing, Bleeding, dying,
   Sealed in the stone cold tomb.

   Refrain

5. Glorious now behold Him arise,
   King and God, and sacrifice;
   Heaven sings Alleluia:
   Alleluia the earth replies.

   Refrain

Swedish Gingerbread Cookies

S*wedish gingerbread cookies are classic for Christmas in Scandinavia. The decorating is the best part—family and friends (and, it's hoped, many children) can spend hours over a single tray! Let them become a tradition.*

7 cups white flour

3 teaspoons baking soda

3 teaspoons ground cinnamon

3 teaspoons ground cloves

3 teaspoons ground ginger

2 cups white sugar

1/2 cup butter, at room temperature

1/2 cup bacon fat, at room
   temperature or another
   1/2 cup butter

1 cup dark (or light) corn syrup

1 1/4 cups heavy cream

1. In a bowl, mix together the flour, baking soda, and spices.

2. Cream the sugar, butter, and bacon fat in a separate bowl. Stir in the corn syrup and heavy cream. Slowly add the dry ingredients and blend well.

3. Flour your hands and toss the dough quickly on a floured surface. Roll into a ball, then divide that into 3 balls. Cover each in waxed paper. Put them in the refrigerator to chill for at least 2 hours.

4. Preheat the oven to 375°F and line baking sheets with parchment paper.

5. Turn the dough out on a lightly floured surface, one ball at a time, and roll out. You can roll the dough pretty thin for crisp cookies. You can also roll the dough directly onto waxed paper.

6. Cut with cookie cutters. Use a spatula to move the shapes onto cookie sheets. You can decorate the cookies with colored sprinkles or sugar crystals before baking, but do not ice.

7. Bake for approximately 12 minutes. (If you have made your cookies thicker, lower the oven temperature to 350°F and bake slightly longer, for 15 to 20 minutes.) When cookies are beginning to brown, remove them from the oven and slide the parchment off the baking sheet. When the cookies have cooled a bit, slide them off the parchment. Cool the cookie sheet before using it again. If you have baked the cookies without decorations, wait until they are completely cool before icing. (See Snow Icing recipe on page 281 and Icing Hints on page 351.)

15 to 30 dozen cookies depending on size and thickness

If you want the cookies to be ornaments, form a hole with a plastic straw or a wooden or metal skewer. For this purpose you can make the cookies thicker and bake them longer at a lower temperature (approximately 25 to 30 minutes at 300°F to 325°F).

Gingerbread House

Follow dough-making instructions on page 36 through step 3 and icing-making instructions on page 281.

If you make your house in accordance with the measurements on the diagram, go to step 1. If you are designing your own, plan out your house carefully ahead of time on parchment or brown construction paper. Be sure it is not too large to fit on your cookie sheets. Cut the paper after you have drawn your measurements and use the cutouts to lay on top of the rolled-out dough.

1. Divide one third of the chilled dough into two pieces and return two thirds to the fridge. Unless you have more than one oven, you'll only be able to bake two pieces at a time, and it's better to keep the extra dough cool in the meantime.

2. Roll out the dough on parchment paper so that you have two large pieces. These will be your front and back sides. *Note: you should roll out this dough thicker than you would for gingerbread cookies, to make sure your walls are strong.*

3. Cut the front and back pieces with a sharp knife, and peel away extra dough.

4. Slide the parchment paper onto a cookie sheet and bake 30 minutes at 325°F. If pieces change shape a little while baking you can trim them right when they come out of the oven and are still warm, but slide the parchment off the cookie sheet first. Let cool.

5. Repeat steps 2-4 for the other two thirds of dough to make your sides and roof.

6. When all your pieces are cool, you can wrap them in plastic wrap and they will keep up to a week.

7. When you are ready, decorate sides with icing, candies, and sprinkles, or whatever else you like, before assembling your Gingerbread House. (See Snow Icing recipe on page 281 and Icing Hints on page 351.)

8. Glue pieces together using chilled icing beaten very stiffly until fluffy and light. Melting a cup or two of sugar down with a little butter will also do the trick. Be sure to build the house on a board it can remain on and use straight pins to anchor your corners while gluing. You can

remove them when the "glue" icing has hardened.

9. Finish decorating roof.

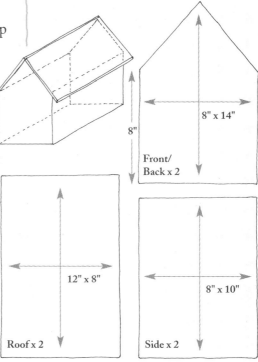

8" x 14"

8"

Front/
Back x 2

12" x 8"

8" x 10"

Roof x 2

Side x 2

Christmas Eve at Sea

John Masefield

A wind is rustling "south and soft,"
 Cooing a quiet country tune,
The calm sea sighs, and far aloft
 The sails are ghostly in the moon.

Unquiet ripples lisp and purr,
 A block there pipes and chirps i' the sheave,
The wheel-ropes jar, the reef-points stir
 Faintly—and it is Christmas Eve.

The hushed sea seems to hold her breath,
 And o'er the giddy, swaying spars,
Silent and excellent as Death,
 The dim blue skies are bright with stars.

Dear God—they shone in Palestine
    Like this, and yon pale moon serene
Looked down among the lowing kine
    On Mary and the Nazarene.

The angels called from deep to deep,
    The burning heavens felt the thrill,
Startling the flocks of silly sheep
    And lonely shepherds on the hill.

To-night beneath the dripping bows,
    Where flashing bubbles burst and throng,
The bow-wash murmurs and sighs and soughs
    A message from the angels' song.

The moon goes nodding down the west,
    The drowsy helmsman strikes the bell;
Rex Judaeorum natus est.
    I charge you, brothers, sing *Nowell,*
Nowell,
Rex Judaeorum natus est.

43

Our Lady's Juggler

Anatole France

In the days of King Louis there was a poor juggler in France, a native of Compiègne, Barnaby by name, who went about from town to town performing feats of skill and strength.

On fair days he would unfold an old worn-out carpet in the public square, and when by means of a jovial address, which he had learned of a very ancient juggler, and which he never varied in the least, he had drawn together the children and loafers, he assumed extraordinary attitudes, and balanced a tin plate on the tip of his nose. At first the crowd would feign indifference.

But when, supporting himself on his hands face downwards, he threw into the air six copper balls, which glittered in the sunshine, and caught them again with his feet; or when throwing himself backwards until his heels and the nape of the neck met, giving his body the form of a perfect wheel, he would juggle in this posture with a dozen knives, a murmur of admiration would escape the spectators, and pieces of money rain down upon the carpet.

Nevertheless, like the majority of those who live by their wits, Barnaby of Compiègne had a great struggle to make a living.

Earning his bread in the sweat of

44

his brow, he bore rather more than his share of the penalties consequent upon the misdoings of our father Adam.

Again, he was unable to work as constantly as he would have been willing to do. The warmth of the sun and the broad daylight were as necessary to enable him to display his brilliant parts as to the trees if flower and fruit should be expected of them. In winter time he was nothing more than a tree stripped of its leaves, and as it were dead. The frozen ground was hard to the juggler, and, like the grasshopper of which Marie de France tells us, the inclement season caused him to suffer both cold and hunger. But as he was simple-natured he bore his ills patiently.

He had never meditated on the origin of wealth, nor upon the inequality of human conditions. He believed firmly that if this life should prove hard, the life to come could not fail to redress the balance, and this hope upheld him. He did not resemble those thievish and miscreant Merry Andrews who sell their souls to the devil. He never blasphemed God's name; he lived uprightly, and although he had no wife of his own, he did not covet his neighbour's, since woman is ever the enemy of the strong man, as it appears by the history of Samson recorded in the Scriptures.

In truth, his was not a nature much disposed to carnal delights, and it was a greater deprivation to him to forsake the tankard than the Hebe who bore it. For whilst not wanting in sobriety, he was fond of a drink when the weather waxed hot. He was a worthy man who feared God, and was very devoted to the Blessed Virgin.

Never did he fail on entering a church to fall upon his knees before the image of the Mother of God, and offer up this prayer to her:

"Blessed Lady, keep watch over my life until it shall please God that I die, and when I am dead, ensure to me the possession of the joys of paradise."

Now on a certain evening after a dreary wet day, as Barnaby pursued his road, sad and bent, carrying under his arm his balls and knives wrapped up in his old carpet, on the watch for some barn where, though he might not sup, he might sleep, he perceived on the road, going in the same direction as himself, a monk, whom he saluted courteously. And as they walked at the same rate they fell into conversation with one another.

"Fellow traveller," said the monk, "how comes it about that you are clothed all in green? Is it perhaps in order to take the part of a jester in some mystery play?"

"Not at all, good father," replied Barnaby. "Such as you see me, I am called Barnaby, and for my calling I am a juggler. There would be no pleasanter calling in the world if it would always provide one with daily bread."

"Friend Barnaby," returned the monk, "be careful what you say. There is no calling more pleasant than the monastic life. Those who lead it are occupied with the praises of God, the Blessed Virgin, and the saints; and, indeed, the religious life is one ceaseless hymn to the Lord."

Barnaby replied—

"Good father, I own that I spoke like an ignorant man. Your calling cannot be in any respect compared to mine, and although there may be some merit in dancing with a penny balanced on a stick on the tip of one's nose, it is not a merit which comes within hail of your own. Gladly would I, like you, good father, sing my office day by day, and especially, the office of the most Holy Virgin, to whom I have vowed a singular devotion. In order to embrace the monastic life I would willingly abandon the art by which from Soissons to Beauvais I am well known in upwards of six hundred towns and villages."

The monk was touched by the juggler's simplicity, and as he was not lacking in discernment, he at once recognized in Barnaby one of those men of whom it is said in the Scriptures: Peace on earth to men of good will. And for this reason he replied—

"Friend Barnaby, come with me, and I will have you admitted into the monastery of which I am Prior. He who guided St. Mary of Egypt in the desert set me upon your path to lead you into the way of salvation."

It was in this manner, then, that

47

Barnaby became a monk. In the monastery into which he was received the religious vied with one another in the worship of the Blessed Virgin, and in her honour each employed all the knowledge and all the skill which God had given him.

The prior on his part wrote books dealing according to the rules of scholarship with the virtues of the Mother of God.

Brother Maurice, with a deft hand copied out these treatises upon sheets of vellum.

Brother Alexander adorned the leaves with delicate miniature paintings. Here were displayed the Queen of Heaven seated upon Solomon's throne, and while four lions were on guard at her feet, around the nimbus which encircled her head hovered seven doves, which are the seven gifts of the Holy Spirit, the gifts, namely, of Fear, Piety, Knowledge, Strength, Counsel, Understanding, and Wisdom. For her companions she had six virgins with hair of gold, namely, Humility, Prudence, Seclusion, Submission, Virginity, and Obedience.

At her feet were two little naked figures, perfectly white, in an attitude of supplication. These were souls imploring her all-powerful intercession for their soul's health, and we may be sure not imploring in vain.

Upon another page facing this, Brother Alexander represented Eve, so that the Fall and the Redemption could be perceived at one and the same time—Eve the Wife abased, and Mary the Virgin exalted.

Furthermore, to the marvel of the beholder, this book contained

48

presentments of the Well of Living Waters, the Fountain, the Lily, the Moon, the Sun, and the Gardens enclosed of which the Song of Songs tells us, the Gate of Heaven and the City of God, and all these things were symbols of the Blessed Virgin.

Brother Marbode was likewise one of the most loving children of Mary.

He spent all his days carving images in stone, so that his beard, his eyebrows, and his hair were white with dust, and his eyes continually swollen and weeping; but his strength and cheerfulness were not diminished, although he was now well gone in years, and it was clear that the Queen of Paradise still cherished her servant in his old age. Marbode represented her seated upon a throne, her brow encircled with an orb-shaped nimbus set with pearls. And he took care that the folds of her dress should cover the feet of her, concerning whom the prophet declared: My beloved is as a garden enclosed.

Sometimes, too, he depicted her in the semblance of a child full of grace, and appearing to say, "Thou art my God, even from my mother's womb."

In the priory, moreover, were poets who composed hymns in Latin, both in prose and verse, in honour of the Blessed Virgin Mary, and amongst the company was even a brother from Picardy who sang the miracles of Our Lady in rhymed verse and in the vulgar tongue.

Being a witness of this emulation in praise and the glorious harvest of their labours, Barnaby mourned his own ignorance and simplicity.

"Alas!" he sighed, as he took his solitary walk in the little shelterless garden of the monastery, "wretched wight that I am, to be unable, like my brothers, worthily to praise the Holy Mother of God, to whom I have vowed my whole heart's affection. Alas! alas! I am but a rough man and unskilled in the arts, and I can render you in service, blessed Lady, neither edifying sermons, nor treatises set out in order according to rule, nor ingenious paintings, nor statues truthfully sculptured, nor verses whose march is measured to the beat of feet. No gift have I, alas!"

After this fashion he groaned and gave himself up to sorrow. But one evening, when the monks were spending their hour of liberty in conversation, he heard one of them tell the tale of a religious man who could repeat nothing other than the Ave Maria. This poor man was despised for his ignorance; but after hi death there issued forth from his mouth five roses in honour of the five letters of the name Mary (Marie), and thus his sanctity was made manifest.

Whilst he listened to this narrative Barnaby marvelled yet

once again at the loving kindness of the Virgin; but the lesson of that blessed death did not avail to console him, for his heart overflowed with zeal, and he longed to advance the glory of his Lady, who is in heaven.

How to compass this he sought but could find no way, and day by day he became the more cast down, when one morning he awakened filled full with joy, hastened to the chapel, and remained there alone for more than an hour. After dinner he returned to the chapel once more.

And, starting from that moment, he repaired daily to the chapel at such hours as it was deserted, and spent within it a good part of the time which the other monks devoted to the liberal and mechanical arts. His sadness vanished, nor did he any longer groan.

A demeanour so strange awakened the curiosity of the monks.

These began to ask one another for what purpose Brother Barnaby could be indulging so persistently in retreat.

The prior, whose duty it is to let nothing escape him in the behaviour of his children in religion, resolved to keep a watch over Barnaby during his

withdrawals to the chapel. One day, then, when he was shut up there after his custom, the prior, accompanied by two of the older monks, went to discover through the chinks in the door what was going on within the chapel.

They saw Barnaby before the alter of the Blessed Virgin, head downwards, with his feet in the air, and he was juggling with six balls of copper and a dozen knives. In honour of the Holy Mother of God he was performing those feats, which aforetime had won him most renown. Not recognizing that the simple fellow was thus placing at the service of the Blessed Virgin his knowledge and skill, the two old monks exclaimed against the sacrilege.

The prior was aware how stainless was Barnaby's soul, but he concluded that he had been seized with madness. They were all three preparing to lead him swiftly from the chapel, when they saw the Blessed Virgin descend the steps of the altar and advance to wipe away with a fold of her azure robe the sweat which was dropping from her juggler's forehead.

Then the prior, falling upon his face upon the pavement, uttered these words—

"Blessed are the simple-hearted, for they shall see God."

"Amen!" responded the old brethren, and kissed the ground.

❄

Joy to the World!

1.

Joy to the World! The Lord is come; Let

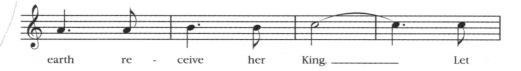

earth re - ceive her King. _____ Let

ev - 'ry ___ heart _____ pre - pare ___ Him ___ room, _____ And

heav'n and na-ture sing, And heav'n and na-ture sing, And

heav'n and heav'n and na-ture sing.

2. Joy to the world! The Saviour reigns;
   Let men their songs employ;
   While fields and floods, rocks, hills
      and plains
   Repeat the sounding joy,
   Repeat the sounding joy,
   Repeat, repeat the sounding joy.

3. He rules the world with truth and
      grace,
   And makes the nations prove
   The glories of His righteousness,
   And wonders of His love,
   And wonders of His love,
   And wonders, and wonders of
      His Love.

55

The Fir Tree

Hans Christian Andersen

Out in the forest stood a pretty little Fir Tree. It had a good place; it could have sunlight, air there was in plenty, and all around grew many larger comrades—pines as well as firs. But the little Fir Tree wished ardently to become greater. It did not care for the warm sun and the fresh air; it took no notice of the peasant children, who went about talking together, when they had come out to look for strawberries and raspberries. Often they came with a whole potful, or had strung berries on a straw; then they would sit down by the little Fir Tree and say, "How pretty and small that one is!" and the Fir Tree did not like to hear that at all.

Next year he had grown a great joint, and the following year he was longer still, for in fir trees one can always tell by the number of rings they have how many years they have been growing.

"Oh, if I were only as great a tree as the others!" sighed the little Fir, "then I would spread my branches far around and look out from my crown into the wide world. The birds would then build nests in my boughs, and when the wind blew I could nod just as grandly as the others yonder."

He took no pleasure in the sunshine, in the birds, and in the red clouds that went sailing over him morning and evening.

When it was winter, the snow lay all around, white and sparkling, a hare would often come jumping along, and spring right over the little Fir Tree. Oh! this made him so angry. But two winters went by, and when the third came the little Tree had grown so tall that the hare was obliged to run around it.

"Oh! to grow, to grow, and become old; that's the only fine thing in the world," thought the Tree.

In the autumn woodcutters always came and felled a few of the largest trees; that was done this year too, and the little Fir Tree, that was now quite well grown, shuddered with fear, for the great stately trees fell to the ground with a crash, and their branches were cut off, so that the trees looked quite naked, long, and slender—they could hardly be recognized. But then they were laid upon wagons, and horses dragged them away out of the wood. Where were they going? What destiny awaited them?

In the spring when the Swallows and the Stork came, the Tree asked them, "Do you know where they were taken? Did you not meet them?"

The Swallows knew nothing about it, but the Stork looked thoughtful, nodded his head, and said:

"Yes, I think so. I met many new ships when I flew out of Egypt; on

59

the ships were stately masts; I fancy these were the trees. They smelled like fir. I can assure you they're stately—very stately."

"Oh that I were only big enough to go over the sea! What kind of thing is this sea, and how does it look?"

"It would take too long to explain all that," said the Stork, and he went away.

"Rejoice in thy youth," said the Sunbeams; "rejoice in thy fresh growth, and in the young life that is within thee."

And the wind kissed the Tree, and the dew wept tears upon it; but the Fir Tree did not understand about that.

When Christmas time approached, quite young trees were felled, sometimes trees which were neither so old nor so large as this fir Tree, that never rested, but always wanted to go away. These young trees, which were always the most beautiful, kept all their branches; they were put upon wagons, and the horses dragged them away out of the wood.

"Where are they all going?" asked the Fir Tree. "They are not greater than I—indeed, one of them was much smaller. Why do they keep all their branches? Whither are they taken?"

"We know that! We know that!" chirped the Sparrows. "Yonder in the town we looked in at the windows. We know where they go. Oh! they are dressed up in the greatest pomp and splendor that can be imagined. We have looked in at the windows, and have perceived that they are planted in the middle of a warm room, and adorned with the most beautiful things—gilt apples, honey cakes,

playthings, and many hundreds of candles."

"And then?" asked the Fir Tree, and trembled through all its branches. "And then? What happens then?"

"Why, we have not seen anything more. But it is incomparable."

"Perhaps I may be destined to tread this glorious path one day!" cried the Fir Tree, rejoicingly. "That is even better than traveling across the sea. How painfully I long for it! If it were only Christmas now! Now I am great and grown up, like the rest who were led away last year. Oh, if I were only on the carriage! If I were only in the warm room, among all the pomp and splendor! And then? Yes, then something even better will come, something far more charming, or else why should they adorn me so? There must be something grander,

something greater still to come; but what? Oh! I'm suffering. I'm longing! I don't know myself what is the matter with me!"

"Rejoice in us," said the Air and Sunshine. "Rejoice in thy fresh youth here in the woodland."

But the Fir Tree did not rejoice at all, but it grew and grew; winter and summer it stood there, green, dark green. The people who saw  it said, "That's a handsome tree!" and at Christmas time it was felled before any of the others. The ax cut deep into its marrow, and the tree fell to the ground with a sigh; it felt pain, a sensation of faintness, and could not think at all of happiness, for it was sad at parting from its home, from the place where it had grown up; it knew that it should never again see the dear old companions, the little bushes and flowers all around—perhaps not even the birds. The parting was not at all agreeable.

The Tree only came to itself when it was unloaded in a yard, with other trees, and heard a man say:

"This one is famous; we want only this one!"

Now two servants came in gay liveries, and carried the Fir Tree into a large, beautiful salon. All around the walls hung pictures, and by the great stove stood large Chinese vases with lions on the covers; there were rocking-chairs, silken sofas, great tables covered with picture-books, and toys worth a hundred times a hundred dollars, at least the children said so. And

the Fir Tree was put into a great tub filled with sand; but no one could see that it was a tub, for it was hung round with green cloth, and stood on a large, many-colored carpet. Oh, how the Tree trembled! What was to happen now? The servants, and the young ladies also, decked it out. On one branch they hung little nets, cut out of colored paper; every net was filled with sweetmeats; golden apples and walnuts hung down, as if they grew there, and more than a hundred little candles, red, white, and blue, were fastened to the different boughs. Dolls that looked exactly like real people—the Tree had never seen such before—swung among the foliage, and high on the summit of the Tree was fixed a tinsel star. It was splendid, particularly splendid.

"This evening," said all, "this

63

evening it will shine."

"Oh," thought the Tree, "that it were evening already! Oh, that the lights may soon be lit up! When may that be done? Will the sparrows fly against the panes? Shall I grow fast here, and stand adorned in summer and winter?"

Yes, he did not guess badly. But he had a complete backache from mere longing, and backache is just as bad for a tree as a headache for a person.

At last the candles were lighted. What a brilliance, what a splendor! The Tree trembled so in all its branches that one of the candles set fire to a green twig, and it was scorched.

"Heaven preserve us!" cried the young ladies; and they hastily put the fire out.

Now the Tree might not even tremble. Oh, that was terrible! It was so afraid of setting fire to some of its ornaments, and it was quite bewildered with all the brilliance. And now the folding doors were thrown wide open, and a number of children rushed in as if they would have overturned the whole Tree; the older people followed more deliberately. The little ones stood quite silent, but only for a minute; then they shouted till the room rang; they danced gleefully round the Tree, and one present after another was plucked from it.

"What are they about?" thought the Tree. "What's going to be done?"

And the candles burned down to the twigs, and as they burned down they were extinguished, and then the children received permission to plunder the Tree. Oh! they rushed in upon it, so that every branch cracked again: if it had not been fastened by the top and by the golden star to the ceiling, it would have fallen down.

The children danced about with their pretty toys. No one looked at the Tree except one old man, who came up and peeped among the branches, but only to see if a fig or an apple had not been forgotten.

"A story! A story!" shouted the children; and they drew a little fat man toward the tree; and he sat down just beneath it—"for then we shall be in the green wood," said he, "and the tree may have the advantage of listening to my tale. But I can only tell one. Will you hear the story of Ivede-Avede, or of Klumpey-Dumpey, who fell down-stairs, and still was raised up to honor and married the Princess?"

"Ivede-Avede!" cried some, "Klumpey-Dumpey!" cried others, and there was a great crying and shouting. Only the Fir Tree was quite silent, and thought, "Shall I not be in it? Shall I have nothing to do in it?" But he had been in the evening's amusement, and had done what was required of him.

And the fat man told about Klumpey-Dumpey who fell downstairs and yet was raised to honor and married a Princess. And the children clapped their hands and cried, "Tell another! Tell another!" and they wanted to hear about Ivede-Avede; but they only got the story of Klumpey-Dumpey. The fir Tree stood quite silent and thoughtful; never had the birds in the wood told such a story as that. Klumpey-Dumpey fell downstairs, and yet came to honor and married a Princess!

"Yes, so it happens in the world!" thought the Fir Tree, and believed it must be true, because that was such a nice man who told it.

"Well, who can know? Perhaps I shall fall downstairs, too, and marry a Princess!" And it looked forward with pleasure to being adorned again, the next evening, with candles and toys, gold and fruit. "Tomorrow I shall not tremble," it thought.

"I shall rejoice in all my splendor. Tomorrow I shall hear the story of Klumpey-Dumpey again, and perhaps that of Ivede-Avede, too."

And the Tree stood all night quiet and thoughtful.

In the morning the servants and the chambermaid came in.

"Now my splendor will begin afresh," thought the Tree. But they dragged him out of the room, and

upstairs to the garret, and here they put him in a dark corner where no daylight shone.

"What's the meaning of this?" thought the Tree. "What am I to do here? What is to happen?"

And he leaned against the wall, and thought, and thought. And he had time enough, for days and nights went by, and nobody came up; and when at length some one came, it was only to put some great boxes in a corner. Now the Tree stood quite hidden away, and the supposition is that it was quite forgotten.

"Now it's winter outside," thought the Tree. "The earth is hard and covered with snow, and people cannot plant me; therefore I suppose I'm to be sheltered here until Spring comes. How considerate that is! How good people are! If it were only not so dark here, and so terribly solitary!—not even a little hare? That was pretty out there in the wood, when the snow lay thick and the hare sprang past; yes, even when he jumped over me; but then I did not like it. It is terribly lonely up here!"

"Piep! piep!" said a little Mouse, and crept forward, and then came another little one. They smelled at the Fir Tree, and then slipped among the branches.

"It's horribly cold," said the two little Mice, "or else it would be comfortable here. Don't you think so, old Fir Tree?"

"I'm not old at all," said the Fir Tree. "There are many much older than I."

"Where do you come from?" asked the Mice. "And what do you know?" They were dreadfully inquisitive. "Tell us about the most beautiful spot on earth. Have you been there? Have you been in the storeroom, where cheeses lie on the shelves, and hams hang from the ceiling, where one dances on tallow candles, and goes in thin and comes out fat?"

"I don't know that," replied the Tree; "but I know the wood, where the sun shines and the birds sing."

And then it told all about its youth.

And the little Mice had never heard anything of the kind; and they listened and said:

"What a number of things you have seen! How happy you must have been!"

"I? replied the Fir Tree; and it thought about what it had told. "Yes, those were really quite happy times." But then he told of the Christmas Eve, when he had been hung with sweetmeats and candles.

"Oh!" said the little Mice, "how

happy you have been, you old Fir Tree!"

"I'm not old at all," said the Tree. "I only came out of the wood this winter. I'm only rather backward in my growth."

"What splendid stories you can tell!" said the little Mice.

And the next night they came with four other little Mice, to hear what the Tree had to relate; and the more it said, the more clearly did it remember everything, and thought, "Those were quite merry days! But they may come again. Klumpey-Dumpey fell downstairs, and yet he married a Princess. Perhaps I shall marry a Princess, too!" And the Fir Tree thought of a pretty little Birch Tree that grew out in the forest; for the Fir Tree, that Birch was a real Princess.

"Who's Klumpey-Dumpey?" asked the little Mice.

And then the Fir Tree told the whole story. It could remember every single word; and the little Mice were ready to leap to the very top of the Tree with pleasure. Next night a great many more Mice came, and on Sunday two Rats even appeared; but these thought the story was not pretty, and the little Mice were sorry for that, for now they also did not like it so much as before.

"Do you know only one story?" asked the Rats.

"Only that one," replied the Tree. "I heard that on the happiest evening of my life; I did not think then how happy I was."

"That's a very miserable story. Don't you know any about bacon and tallow candles—a storeroom story?"

"No," said the Tree.

"Then we'd rather not hear

68

you," said the Rats.

And they went back to their own people. The little Mice at last stayed away also; and then the Tree sighed and said:

"It was very nice when they sat round me, the merry little Mice, and listened when I spoke to them. Now that's past too. But I shall remember to be pleased when they take me out."

But when did that happen? Why, it was one morning that people came and rummaged in the garret; the boxes were put away, and the tree brought out; they certainly threw him rather roughly on the floor, but a servant dragged him away at once to the stairs, where the daylight shone.

"Now life is beginning again!" thought the Tree.

It felt the fresh air and the first sunbeam, and now it was out in the courtyard. Everything passed so quickly that the Tree quite forgot to look at itself, there was so much to look at all round. The courtyard was close to a garden, and here everything was blooming; the roses hung fresh over the paling, the linden trees were in blossom, and the swallows cried, "Quinze-wit! quinze-wit! my husband's come!" But it was not the Fir Tree they meant.

"Now I shall live!" said the Tree, rejoicingly, and spread its branches far out; but, alas! they were all withered and yellow; and it lay in the corner among nettles and weeds. The tinsel star was still upon it, and shone in the bright sunshine.

In the courtyard a couple of the merry

children were playing who had danced round the tree at Christmas time, and had rejoiced over it. One of the youngest ran up and tore off the golden star.

"Look what is sticking to the ugly old fir tree!" said the child, and he trod upon the branches till they cracked again under his boots.

And the Tree looked at all the blooming flowers and the splendor of the garden, and then looked at itself, and wished it had remained in the dark corner of the garret; it thought of its fresh youth in the wood, of the merry Christmas Eve, and of the little Mice which had listened so pleasantly to the story of Klumpey-Dumpey.

"Past! past!" said the old Tree. "Had I but rejoiced when I could have done so! Past! past!"

And the servant came and chopped the Tree into little pieces; a whole bundle lay there; it blazed brightly under the great brewing copper, and it sighed deeply, and each sigh was like a little shot; and the children who were at play there ran up and seated themselves at the fire, looked into it, and cried "Puff! puff!" But at each explosion, which was a deep sigh, the Tree thought of a summer day in the woods, or of a winter night there, when the stars beamed; he thought of Christmas Eve and of Klumpey-Dumpey, the only story he had ever heard or knew how to tell; and then the Tree was burned.

The boys played in the garden, and the youngest had on his breast a golden star, which the Tree had worn on its happiest evening. Now that was past, and the Tree's life was past, and the story is past too: past! past!—and that's the way with all stories. ❄

Cinnamon Bun Christmas Tree

T*his is the coziest way to have Christmas day breakfast. You can bake the buns in advance and, if you do, let them cool before wrapping in plastic and storing in the freezer. On Christmas morning, unwrap and pop them in the oven at 250°F degrees for 20 minutes.*

DOUGH:
2 packages active dry yeast
1 cup warm milk
3$1/2$ cups flour
$1/2$ cup (1 stick) butter
$1/4$ cup white sugar
3 egg yolks
$1/2$ cup golden raisins (optional)
$1/4$ cup pecan halves (optional)
1 grated lemon rind
2 teaspoons melted butter
1 cup sugar mixed with
    2 teaspoons cinnamon

HONEY GLAZE:
Cream together:
$1/4$ cup butter
1 cup confectioners' sugar
$1/4$ cup honey

WHITE ICING:
Mix together:
$1/4$ cup confectioners' sugar
1$1/2$ tablespoons water

1. Dissolve yeast in warm milk. Mix in $1/2$ cup flour. Cover and put in warm place to rise (about 20 minutes).

2. Cream together butter and ¼ cup sugar. Mix in egg yolks one at a time. Gradually add remaining 3 cups flour, then raisins, pecans, and lemon rind.

3. Once yeast mixture has risen, add to dough and blend well. Knead until dough is smooth (about 7 minutes).

4. Lightly brush dough with vegetable oil. Place in bowl, cover with kitchen towel, and put in warm place. Let rise to twice its size (about 45 minutes).

5. Punch down dough and cover. Let rise another 30 to 40 minutes.

6. Punch down dough again. Cut in half. Roll each piece into a rectangle 12 x 18 inches. Brush each with melted butter (saving a little), then sprinkle entire surface with cinnamon and remaining cup of sugar. Taking longest end, roll tightly. Place seam side down; slice buns ½-inch thick.

7. Place four buns in a row near bottom of cookie sheet. Place three buns above this row so that each one nestles between tops of buns below. Do same for another row of two buns. Top off with one bun. Place a bun beneath center of bottom row for tree stump. Cover tree with kitchen towel. Set aside to rise for 30 minutes.

8. Preheat oven to 350°F. Brush remaining melted butter on tree. Bake for 30 minutes or until dough turns golden brown. Remove and let rest five minutes. Spread Honey Glaze on top. When nearly cool, drizzle White Icing on top.

1 tree of 11 buns

The Mahogany Tree

William Makepeace Thackeray

Christmas is here:
Winds whistle shrill,
Icy and chill,
Little care we:
Little we fear
Weather without,
Sheltered about
The Mahogany Tree.

Once on the boughs
Birds of rare plume
Sang, in its bloom;
Night-birds are we:

Here we carouse,
Singing like them,
Perched round the stem
Of the jolly old tree.

Here let us sport,
Boys, as we sit;
Laughter and wit
Flashing so free.
Life is but short—
When we are gone,
Let them sing on,
Round the old tree.

Evenings we knew,
Happy as this;
Faces we miss,
Pleasant to see.
Kind hearts and true,
Gentle and just,
Peace to your dust!
We sing round the tree.

Care, like a dun,
Lurks at the gate:
Let the dog wait;
Happy we'll be!
Drink, every one;
Pile up the coals,
Fill the red bowls,
Round the old tree!

Drain we the cup.—
Friend, art afraid?
Spirits are laid
In the Red Sea.
Mantle it up;
Empty it yet;
Let us forget,
Round the old tree.

Sorrows, begone!
Life and its ills,
Duns and their bills,
Bid we to flee.
Come with the dawn,
Blue-devil sprite,
Leave us to-night,
Round the old tree.

75

O Come, All Ye Faithful

1.

O Come, All Ye Faith - ful, Joy - ful and tri - umph - ant, O

come ye, O come __ ye to Beth - le - hem.

Come and be - hold Him, Born the King of An - gels. O

Refrain

come, let us a - dore Him, O come, let us a - dore Him, O come, let us a - dore Him, ___ Christ, ___ the Lord.

2. Sing, choirs of angels, sing in exultation,
   O sing, all ye citizens of heav'n above!
   Glory to God, all Glory in the highest;

   Refrain

3. Yea, Lord, we greet Thee, born this happy morning,
   Jesus, to Thee be all glory giv'n;
   Word of the Father, Now in flesh appearing;

   Refrain

The Miraculous Staircase

Arthur Gordon

On that cool December morning in 1878, sunlight lay like an amber rug across the dusty streets and adobe houses of Santa Fe. It glinted on the bright tile roof of the almost completed Chapel of Our Lady of light and on the nearby windows of the convent school run by the Sisters of Loretto. Inside the convent, the Mother Superior looked up from her packing as a tap came on her door.

"It's *another* carpenter, Reverend Mother," said Sister Francis Louise, her round face apologetic. "I told him that you're leaving right away, that you haven't time to see him, but he says. . . ."

"I know what he says," Mother Magdalene said, going on resolutely with her packing. "That he's heard about our problem with the new chapel. That he's the best carpenter in all of New Mexico. That he can build us a staircase to the choir loft despite the fact that the brilliant architect in Paris who drew the plans failed to leave any space for one. And despite the fact that five master carpenters have already tried and failed. You're quite right, Sister; I don't have time to listen to that story again."

"But he seems such a nice man," said Sister Francis Louise wistfully, "and he's out there with his burro, and. . . ."

"I'm sure," said Mother Magdalene with a smile, "that he's a charming man, and that his burro is a charming donkey. But there's sickness down at the Santo Domingo pueblo, and it may be cholera. Sister Mary Helen and I are the only ones here who've had cholera. So we have to go. And you have to stay and run the school. And that's that!" Then she called, "Manuela!"

A young Indian girl of 12 or 13, black-haired and smiling, came in quietly on moccasined feet. She was a mute. She could hear and understand, but the Sisters had been unable to teach her to speak. The Mother Superior spoke to her gently: "Take my things down to the wagon, child. I'll be right there." And to sister Francis Louise:

"You'd better tell your carpenter friend to come back in two or three weeks. I'll see him then."

"Two or three weeks! Surely you'll be home for Christmas?"

"If it's the Lord's will, Sister. I hope so."

In the street, beyond the waiting wagon, Mother Magdalene could see the carpenter, a bearded man, strongly built and taller than most Mexicans, with dark eyes and a smiling, wind-burned face. Beside him, laden with tools and scraps of

lumber, a small gray burro stood patiently. Manuela was stroking its nose, glancing shyly at its owner. "You'd better explain," said the Mother Superior, "that the child can hear him, but she can't speak."

Goodbyes were quick—the best kind when you leave a place you love. Southwest, then, along the dusty trail, the mountains purple with shadow, the Rio Grande a ribbon of green far off to the right. The pace was slow, but Mother Magdalene and Sister Mary Helen amused themselves by singing songs and telling Christmas stories as the sun marched up and down the sky. And their leathery driver listened

and nodded.

Two days of this brought them to Santo Domingo Pueblo, where the sickness was not cholera after all, but measles, almost as deadly in an Indian village. And so they stayed, helping the harassed Father Sebastian, visiting the dark adobe hovels where feverish brown children tossed and fierce Indian dogs showed their teeth.

At night they were bone-weary, but sometimes Mother Magdalene found time to talk to Father Sebastian about her plans for he dedication of the new chapel. It was to be in April; the Archbishop himself would be there. And it might have been dedicated sooner, were it not for this incredible business of a choir loft with no means of access—unless it were a ladder.

"I told the Bishop," said Mother

Magdalene, "that it would be a mistake to have the plans drawn in Paris. If something went wrong, what could we do? But he wanted our chapel in Santa Fe patterned after the Sainte Chapelle in Paris, and who am I to argue with Bishop Lamy? So the talented Monsieur Mouly designs a beautiful choir loft high up under the rose window, and no way to get to it."

"Perhaps," sighed Father Sebastian, "he had in mind a heavenly choir. The kind with wings."

"It's not funny," said Mother Magdalene a bit sharply. "I've prayed and prayed, but apparently there's no solution at all. There just isn't room on the chapel floor for the supports such a staircase needs."

The days passed, and with each passing day Christmas drew closer. Twice, horsemen on their way from Santa Fe to Albuquerque brought letters from Sister Francis Louise. All was well at the convent, but Mother Magdalene frowned over certain paragraphs. "The children are getting ready for Christmas," Sister Francis Louise wrote in her first letter. "Our little Manuela and the carpenter have become great friends. It's amazing how much he seems to know about us all. . . ."

And what, thought Mother Magdalene, is the carpenter still doing there?

The second letter also mentioned the carpenter. "Early every morning he comes with another load of lumber, and every night he goes away. When we ask him by what authority he does these things, he smiles and says nothing. We have tried to pay him for his work, but he will accept no pay. . . ."

Work? What work? Mother Magdalene wrinkled up her nose in exasperation. Had that soft-hearted Sister Francis Louise given the man permission to putter around in the new chapel? With firm and disapproving hand, the Mother Superior wrote a note ordering an end to all such unauthorized activities. She gave it to an Indian pottery-maker on his way to Santa Fe.

But that night the first snow fell, so thick and heavy that the Indian turned back. Next day at noon the sun shone again on a world glittering with diamonds. But Mother Magdalene knew that another snowfall might make it impossible for her to be home for Christmas. By now the sickness at Santo Domingo was subsiding. And so that afternoon they began the long ride back.

The snow did come again, making their slow progress even slower. It was late on Christmas Eve, close to midnight, when the tired horses plodded up to the convent door. But lamps still burned. Manuela flew down the steps, Sister Francis Louise close behind her. And chilled and weary though she was, Mother Magdalene sensed instantly an excitement, an electricity in the air that she could not understand.

Nor did she understand it when they led her, still in her heavy wraps, down the corridor, into the new, as-yet-unused chapel where a few candles burned. "Look, Reverend Mother," breathed Sister Francis Louise. "Look!"

Like a curl of smoke the staircase rose before them, as insubstantial as a dream. Its top rested against the choir loft. Nothing else supported it; it seemed to float on air. There were no banisters. Two complete spirals it made, the polished wood gleaming softly in the candlelight. "Thirty-three steps," whispered Sister Francis Louise. "One for each year in the life of Our Lord."

Mother Magdalene moved forward like a woman in a trance. She put her foot on the first step, then the second, then the third. There was not a tremor. She looked down, bewildered, at Manuela's ecstatic, upturned face. "But it's impossible! There wasn't time!"

"He finished yesterday," the Sister said. "He didn't come today. No one has seen him anywhere in Santa Fe. He's gone."

"But *who* was he? Don't you even know his *name*?"

The Sister shook her head, but now Manuela pushed forward, nodding emphatically. Her mouth opened; she took a deep, shuddering breath; she made a sound that was like a gasp in the stillness. The nuns stared at her, transfixed. She tried again. This time it was a syllable, followed by another. "Jo-sé." She clutched the Mother Superior's arm and repeated the first word she had ever spoken. "José!"

Sister Francis Louise crossed herself. Mother Magdalene felt her heart contract. José—the Spanish word for Joseph. Joseph the Carpenter. Joseph the Master Woodworker of. . . .

"José!" Manuela's dark eyes were full of tears. "José!"

Silence, then, in the shadowy chapel. No one moved. Far away across the snow-silvered town Mother Magdalene heard a bell tolling midnight. She came down the stairs and took Manuela's hand. She felt uplifted by a great surge of wonder and gratitude and compassion and love. And she knew what it was. It was the spirit of Christmas. And it was upon them all.

Author's Note. You may see the inexplicable staircase itself in Santa Fe today. It stands just as it stood when the chapel was dedicated almost a hundred years ago—except for the banister, which was added later. Tourists stare and marvel. Architects shake their heads and murmur, "Impossible." No one knows the identity of the designer-builder. All the Sisters know is that the problem existed, a stranger came, solved it and left.

The 33 steps make two complete turns without central support. There are no nails in the staircase; only wooden pegs. The curved stringers are put together with exquisite precision; the wood is spliced in seven places on the inside and nice on the outside. The wood is said to be a hard-fir variety, nonexistent in New Mexico. School records show that no payment for the staircase was ever made.

Christmas Greeting from a Fairy to a Child

Lewis Carroll

Lady, dear, if Fairies may
    For a moment lay aside
Cunning tricks and elfish play,
    'Tis at happy Christmas-tide.

We have heard the children say—
    Gentle children, whom we love—
Long ago on Christmas Day,
    Came a message from above.

Still, as Christmas-tide comes round,
    They remember it again—
Echo still the joyful sound,
    "Peace on earth, good-will to men!"

Yet the hearts must childlike be
    Where such heavenly guests abide;
Unto children, in their glee,
    All the year is Christmas-tide!

Thus, forgetting tricks and play
    For a moment, Lady dear,
We would wish you, if we may,
    Merry Christmas, glad New Year!

The Birds' Christmas Carol

Kate Douglas Wiggin

I. A Little Snow Bird

It was very early Christmas morning, and in the stillness of the dawn, with the soft snow falling on the house-tops, a little child was born in the Bird household.

They had intended to name the baby Lucy, if it were a girl; but they had not expected her on Christmas morning, and a real Christmas baby was not to be lightly named—the whole family agreed in that.

They were consulting about it in the nursery. Mr. Bird said that he had assisted in naming the three boys, and that he should leave this matter entirely to Mrs. Bird; Donald wanted the child called "Dorothy," after a pretty, curly-haired girl who sat next to him in school; Paul chose "Luella," for Luella was the nurse who had been with him during his whole babyhood, up to the time of his first trousers, and the name suggested all sorts of comfortable things. Uncle Jack said that the first girl should always be named for her mother, no matter how hideous the name happened to be.

Grandma said that she would prefer not to take any part in the discussion, and everybody suddenly remembered that Mrs. Bird had thought of naming the baby Lucy, for Grandma herself; and, while it would be indelicate for her to favor that name, it would be against human nature for her to suggest any other, under the circumstances.

Hugh, the "hitherto baby," if that is a possible term, sat in one corner and said nothing, but felt, in some mysterious way, that his nose was out of joint; for there was a newer baby now, a possibility he had never taken into consideration; and the "first girl," too,—a still higher development of treason, which made him actually green with jealousy.

But it was too profound a subject to be settled then and there, on the spot; besides, Mamma had not been asked, and everybody felt it rather absurd, after all, to forestall a decree that was certain to be absolutely wise, just, and perfect.

The reason that the subject had been brought up at all so early in the day lay in the fact that Mrs. Bird never allowed her babies to go over night unnamed. She was a person of so great decision of character that she would have blushed at such a thing; she said that to let blessed babies go dangling and dawdling about without names, for months and months, was enough to ruin them for life. She also said that if one could not make up one's mind in twenty-four hours it was a sign that—But I will not repeat the rest, as it might prejudice you against the most charming woman in the world.

So Donald took his new velocipede and went out to ride up and down the stone pavement and notch the shins of innocent people as they passed by, while Paul spun his musical top on the front steps.

But Hugh refused to leave the scene of action. He seated himself on the top stair in the hall, banged his head against the railing a few times, just by way of uncorking the vials of his wrath, and then subsided into gloomy silence, waiting to declare war if more "first girl babies" were thrust upon a family already surfeited with that unnecessary article.

Meanwhile dear Mrs. Bird lay in her room, weak, but safe and happy, with her sweet girl baby by her side and the heaven of motherhood opening again before her. Nurse was making gruel in the

kitchen, and the room was dim and quiet. There was a cheerful open fire in the grate, but though the shutters were closed, the side windows that looked out on the Church of Our Saviour, next door, were a little open.

Suddenly a sound of music poured out into the bright air and drifted into the chamber. It was the boy choir singing Christmas anthems. Higher and higher rose the clear, fresh voices, full of hope and cheer, as children's voices always are. Fuller and fuller grew the burst of melody as one glad strain fell upon another in joyful harmony:—

> "Carol, brothers, carol,
>   Carol joyfully,
>   Carol the good tidings,
>   Carol merrily!
> And pray a gladsome Christmas

For all your fellow-men:
Carol, brothers, carol,
   Christmas Day again."

One verse followed another,
always with the same sweet
refrain:—

"And pray a gladsome Christmas
   For all your fellow-men:
Carol, brothers, carol,
   Christmas Day again."

Mrs. Bird thought, as the music
floated in upon her gentle sleep,
that she had slipped into heaven
with her new baby, and that the
angels were bidding them welcome.
But the tiny bundle by her side
stirred a little, and though it was
scarcely more than the ruffling of
a feather, she awoke; for the
mother-ear is so close to the heart
that it can hear the faintest

whisper of a child.

She opened her eyes and drew
the baby closer. It looked like a rose
dipped in milk, she thought, this
pink and white blossom of girlhood,
or like a pink cherub, with its halo
of pale yellow hair, finer than
floss silk.

"Carol, brothers, carol,
   Carol joyfully,
Carol the good tidings,
   Carol merrily!"

The voices were brimming over
with joy.

"Why, my baby," whispered Mrs.
Bird in soft surprise, "I had
forgotten what day it was. You are
a little Christmas child, and we will
name you 'Carol'—mother's
Christmas Carol!"

"What!" said Mr. Bird, coming
in softly and closing the door

91

behind him.

"Why, Donald, don't you think 'Carol' is a sweet name for a Christmas baby? It came to me just a moment ago in the singing, as I was lying here half asleep and half awake."

"I think it is a charming name, dear heart, and sounds just like you, and I hope that, being a girl, this baby has some chance of being as lovely as her mother;"—at which speech from the baby's papa Mrs. Bird, though she was as weak and tired as she could be, blushed with happiness.

And so Carol came by her name.

Of course, it was thought foolish by many people, though Uncle Jack declared laughingly that it was very strange if a whole family of Birds could not be indulged in a single Carol; and Grandma, who adored the child, thought the name much

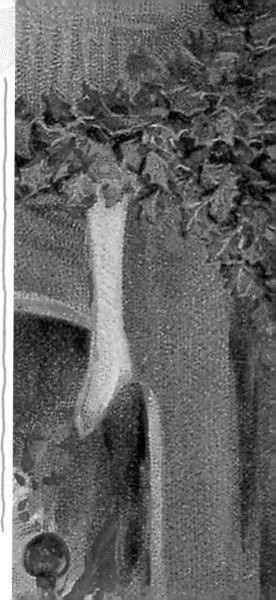

more appropriate than Lucy, but was glad that people would probably think it short for Caroline.

Perhaps because she was born in holiday time, Carol was a very happy baby. Of course, she was too tiny to understand the joy of Christmas-tide, but people say there is everything in a good beginning, and she may have breathed in unconsciously the fragrance of evergreens and holiday dinners; while the peals of sleigh-bells and the laughter of happy children may have fallen upon her baby ears and wakened in them a glad surprise at the merry world she had come to live in.

Her cheeks and lips were as red as holly-berries; her hair was for all the world the color of a Christmas candle-flame; her eyes were bright as stars; her laugh like a chime of Christmas-bells, and her tiny hands forever outstretched in giving.

Such a generous little creature you never saw! A spoonful of bread and milk had always to be taken by Mamma or nurse before Carol could enjoy her supper; whatever bit of cake or sweetmeat found its way into her pretty fingers was straightway broken in half to be shared with Donald, Paul, or Hugh; and when they made believe nibble the morsel with affected enjoyment, she would clap her hands and crow with delight.

"Why does she do it?" asked Donald thoughtfully. "None of us boys ever did."

"I hardly know," said Mamma, catching her darling to her heart, "except that she is a little Christmas child, and so she has a tiny share of the blessedest birthday the world ever knew!"

II. Drooping Wings

It was December, ten years later.

Carol had seen nine Christmas trees lighted on her birthdays, one after another; nine times she had assisted in the holiday festivities of the household, though in her babyhood her share of the gayeties was somewhat limited.

For five years, certainly, she had

hidden presents for Mamma and Papa in their own bureau drawers, and harbored a number of secrets sufficiently large to burst a baby brain, had it not been for the relief gained by whispering them all to Mamma, at night, when she was in her crib, a proceeding which did not in the least lessen the value of a secret in her innocent mind.

For five years she had heard "'Twas the night before Christmas," and hung up a scarlet stocking many sizes too large for her, and pinned a sprig of holly on her little white nightgown, to show Santa Claus that she was a "truly" Christmas child, and dreamed of fur-coated saints and toy-packs and reindeer, and wished everybody a "Merry Christmas" before it was light in the morning, and lent every one of her new toys to the neighbors' children before noon, and eaten turkey and plum-pudding, and gone to bed at night in a trance of happiness at the day's pleasures.

Donald was away at college now. Paul and Hugh were great manly fellows, taller than their mother. Papa Bird had gray hairs in his whiskers; and Grandma, God bless her, had been four Christmases in heaven.

But Christmas in the Birds' Nest was scarcely as merry now as it used to be in the bygone years, for the little child, that once brought such an added blessing to the day, lay month after month a patient, helpless invalid, in the room where she was born. She had never been very strong in body, and it was with a pang of terror her mother and father noticed, soon after she was five years old, that she began to limp, ever so slightly; to complain too often of weariness, and to nestle close to her mother, saying she "would rather not go out to play, please." The illness was slight at first, and hope was always stirring in Mrs. Bird's heart. "Carol would feel stronger in the summer-time"; or, "She would be better when she had spent a year in the country;" or, "She would outgrow it"; or, "They would try a new physician"; but by and by it came to be all too sure that no physician save One could make Carol strong again, and that no "summer-time" nor "country air," unless it were the everlasting

summer-time in a heavenly country, could bring back the little

girl to health.

The cheeks and lips that were once as red as hollyberries faded to faint pink; the star-like eyes grew softer, for they often gleamed through tears; and the gay child-laugh, that had been like a chime of Christmas bells, gave place to a smile so lovely, so touching, so tender and patient, that it filled every corner of the house with a gentle radiance that might have come from the face of the Christ-child himself.

Love could do nothing; and when we have said that we have said all, for it is stronger than anything else in the whole wide world. Mr. and Mrs. Bird were talking it over one evening, when all the children were asleep. A famous physician had visited them that day, and told them that some time, it might be in one year, it

might be in more, Carol would slip quietly off into heaven, whence she came.

"It is no use to close our eyes to it any longer," said Mr. Bird, as he paced up and down the library floor; "Carol will never be well again. It almost seems as if I could not bear it when I think of that loveliest child doomed to lie there day after day, and, what is still more, to suffer pain that we are helpless to keep away from her. Merry Christmas, indeed; it gets to

be the saddest day in the year to me!" and poor Mr. Bird sank into a chair by the table, and buried his face in his hands to keep his wife from seeing the tears that would come in spite of all his efforts.

"But, Donald, dear," said sweet Mrs. Bird, with trembling voice, "Christmas Day may not be so merry with us as it used, but it is very happy, and that is better, and very blessed, and that is better yet. I suffer chiefly for Carol's sake, but I have almost given up being sorrowful for my own. I am too happy in the child, and I see too clearly what she has done for us and the other children. Donald and Paul and Hugh were three strong, willful, boisterous boys, but now you seldom see such tenderness, devotion, thought for others, and self-denial in lads of their years. A quarrel or a hot word is almost unknown in this house, and why? Carol would hear it, and it would distress her, she is so full of love and goodness. The boys study with all their might and main. Why? Partly, at least, because they like to teach Carol, and amuse her by telling her what they read. When the seamstress comes, she likes to sew in Miss Carol's room, because there she forgets her own troubles, which, Heaven knows, are sore enough! And as for me, Donald, I am a better woman every day for Carol's sake; I have to be her eyes, ears, feet, hands,—her strength, her hope; and she, my own little child, is my example!"

"I was wrong, dear heart," said Mr. Bird more cheerfully; "we will try not to repine, but to rejoice instead, that we have an 'angel of the house.'"

❄

Hark! The Herald Angels Sing

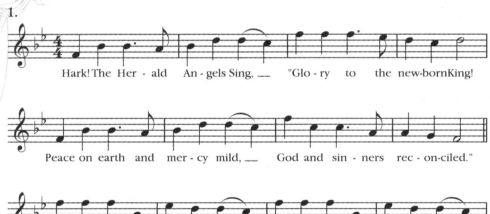

1.

Hark! The Her - ald An - gels Sing, __ "Glo - ry to the new-bornKing!

Peace on earth and mer - cy mild, __ God and sin - ners rec - on-ciled."

Joy - ful all ye na - tions rise, __ Join the tri - umph of the skies; __

With th'an-gel-ic host pro-claim, "Christ is — born in Beth-le-hem."

Refrain

Hark the Her-ald An-gels Sing, "Glo-ry — to the new-born King!"

2. Christ, by highest heaven adored;
   Christ, the everlasting Lord;
   Come, Desire of Nations, come,
   Fix in us thy humble home.
   Veiled in flesh the Godhead see;
   Hail th'Incarnate Deity,
   Pleased as man with man to dwell;
   Jesus, our Emmanuel

   Refrain

3. Hail, the heave'nborn Prince of Peace!
   Hail, the Sun of Righteousness!
   Light and life to all He brings,
   Ris'n with healing in His wing;
   Mild He lays His glory by,
   Born that man no more may die,
   Born to raise the sons of earth,
   Born to give them second birth;

   Refrain

The Legend of the Christmas Rose

Selma Lagerlöf

Robber Mother, who lived in Robbers' Cave up in Göinge forest, went down to the village one day on a begging tour. Robber Father, who was an outlawed man, did not dare to leave the forest. She took with her five youngsters, and each youngster bore a sack on his back as long as himself. When Robber Mother stepped inside the door of a cabin, no one dared refuse to give her whatever she demanded; for she was not above coming back the following night and setting fire to the house if she had not been well received. Robber Mother and her brood were worse than a pack of wolves, and many a man felt like running a spear through them; but it was never done, because they all knew that the man stayed up in the forest, and he would have known how to wreak vengeance if anything had happened to the children or the old woman.

Now that Robber Mother went from house to house and begged, she came to Övid, which at that time was a cloister. She rang the bell of the cloister gate and asked for food. The watchman let down a small wicket in the gate and handed her six round bread cakes—one for herself and one for each of the five children.

While the mother was standing quietly at the gate, her youngsters were running about. And now one of them came and pulled at her skirt, as a signal that he had discovered something which she ought to come and see, and Robber Mother followed him promptly.

The entire cloister was surrounded by a high and strong wall, but the youngster had managed to find a little back gate which stood ajar. When Robber Mother got there, she pushed the gate open and walked inside without asking leave, as it was her custom to do.

Övid Cloister was managed at that time by Abbot Hans, who knew all about herbs. Just within the cloister wall he had planted a little herb garden, and it was into this that the old woman had forced her way.

At first glance Robber Mother was so astonished that she paused at the gate. It was high summertide, and Abbot Hans' garden was so full of flowers that the eyes were fairly dazzled by the blues, reds, and yellows, as one looked into it. But presently an indulgent smile spread over her features, and she started to walk up a narrow path that lay between many flower beds.

In the garden a lay brother walked about, pulling up weeds. It was he who had left the door in the wall open, that he might throw the weeds and tares on the rubbish heap outside.

When he saw Robber Mother coming in, with all five youngsters in tow, he ran toward her at once and ordered them away. But the beggar woman walked right on as before. The lay brother knew of no other remedy than to run into the cloister and call for help.

He returned with two stalwart monks, and Robber Mother saw that now it meant business! She let out a perfect volley of shrieks, and, throwing herself upon the monks, clawed and bit at them; so did all the youngsters. The men soon learned that she could overpower them, and all they could do was go back into the cloister for reinforcements.

As they ran through the passageway which led to the cloister, they met Abbot Hans, who came rushing out to learn what all this noise was about.

He upbraided them for using force and forbade their calling for help. He sent both monks back to their work, and although he was an old and fragile man, he took with him only the lay brother.

He came up to the woman and asked in a mild tone if the garden pleased her.

Robber Mother turned defiantly toward Abbot Hans, for she expected only to be trapped and overpowered. But when she noticed his white hair and bent form, she answered peaceably, "First, when I saw this, I thought I had never seen a prettier garden; but now I see that it can't be compared with one I know of. If you could see the garden of which I am thinking you would uproot all the flowers

planted here and cast them away like weeds."

The Abbot's assistant was hardly less proud of the flowers than the Abbot himself, and after hearing her remarks he laughed derisively.

Robber Mother grew crimson with rage to think that her word was doubted, and she cried out: "You monks, who are holy men, certainly must know that on every Christmas Eve the great Göinge forest is transformed into a beautiful garden, to commemorate the hour of our Lord's birth. We who live in the forest have seen this happen every year. And in that garden I have seen flowers so lovely that I dared not life my hand to pluck them."

Ever since his childhood, Abbot Hans had heard it said that on every Christmas Eve the forest was dressed in holiday glory. He had often longed to see it, but he had never had the good fortune. Eagerly he begged and implored Robber Mother that he might come up to the Robbers' Cave on Christmas Eve. If she would only send one of her children to show him the way, he could ride up there alone, and he would never betray them—on the contrary, he would reward them insofar as it lay in his power.

Robber Mother said no at first, for she was thinking of Robber Father and of the peril which might befall him should she permit Abbot Hans to ride up to their cave. At the same time the desire to prove to the monk that the garden which she knew was more beautiful than his got the better of her, and she gave in.

107

"But more than one follower you cannot take with you," said she, "and you are not to waylay us or trap us, as sure as you are a holy man."

This Abbot Hans promised, and then Robber Mother went her way.

It happened that Archbishop Absalon from Lund came to Övid and remained through the night. The lay brother heard Abbot Hans telling the Bishop about Robber Father and asking him for a letter of ransom for the man, that he might lead an honest life among respectable folk.

But the Archbishop replied that he did not care to let the robber loose among honest folk in the villages. It would be best for all that he remain in the forest.

Then Abbot Hans grew zealous and told the Bishop all about Göinge forest, which, every year at Yuletide, clothed itself in summer bloom around the Robbers' Cave. "If these bandits are not so bad but that God's glories can be made manifest to them, surely we cannot be too wicked to experience the same blessing."

The Archbishop knew how to answer Abbot Hans. "This much I will promise you, Abbot Hans," he said, smiling, "that any day you send me a blossom from the garden in Göinge forest, I will give you letters of ransom for all the outlaws you may choose to plead for."

The following Christmas Eve Abbot Hans was on his way to the forest. One of the Robber Mother's wild youngsters ran ahead of him, and close behind him was the lay brother.

It turned out to be a long and hazardous ride. They climbed steep and slippery side paths, crawled over swamp and marsh, and pushed through windfall and bramble. Just as daylight was waning, the robber boy guided them across a forest meadow, skirted by tall, naked leaf trees and green fir trees. Back of the meadow loomed a mountain wall, and in this wall they saw a door of thick boards. Now Abbot Hans understood that they had arrived, and dismounted. The child opened the heavy door for him, and he looked into a poor mountain grotto, with bare stone walls. Robber Mother was seated before a log fire that burned in the middle of the floor. Alongside the walls were beds of virgin pine and moss, and on one of these beds lay Robber Father asleep.

"Come in, you out there!" shouted Robber Mother without rising, "and fetch the horses in with you, so they won't be destroyed by the night cold."

Abbot Hans walked boldly into the cave, and the lay brother followed. Here were wretchedness and poverty! and nothing was done to celebrate Christmas.

Robber Mother spoke in a tone as haughty and dictatorial as any well-to-do peasant woman. "Sit down by the fire and warm yourself, Abbot Hans," said she; "and if you have food with you, eat, for the food which we in the forest prepare you wouldn't care to taste. And if you are tired after the long journey, you can lie down on one of these beds to sleep. You needn't be afraid of oversleeping, for I'm sitting here by

109

the fire keeping watch. I shall awaken you in time to see that which you have come up here to see."

Abbot Hans obeyed Robber Mother and brought forth his food sack; but he was so fatigued after the journey he was hardly able to eat, and as soon as he could stretch himself on the bed, he fell asleep.

The lay brother was also assigned a bed to rest and he dropped into a doze.

When he woke up, he saw that Abbot Hans had left his bed and was sitting by the fire talking with Robber Mother. The outlawed robber sat also by the fire. He was a tall, raw-boned man with a dull, sluggish appearance. His back was turned to Abbot Hans, as though he would have it appear that he was not listening to the conversation.

Abbot Hans was telling Robber Mother all about the Christmas preparations he had seen on the journey, reminding her of Christmas feasts and games which she must have known in her youth, when she lived at peace with mankind.

At first Robber Mother answered in short, gruff sentences, but by degrees she became more subdued and listened more intently. Suddenly Robber Father turned toward Abbot Hans and shook his clenched fist in his face. "You miserable monk! did you come here to coax from me my wife and children? Don't you know that I

am an outlaw and may not leave the forest?"

Abbot Hans looked him fearlessly in the eyes. "It is my purpose to get a letter of ransom for you from Archbishop Absalon," said he. He had hardly finished speaking when the robber and his wife burst out laughing. They knew well enough the kind of mercy a forest robber could expect from Bishop Absalon!

"Oh, if I get a letter of ransom from Absalon," said Robber Father, "then I'll promise you that never again will I steal so much as a goose."

Suddenly Robber Mother rose.

"You sit here and talk, Abbot Hans," she said, "so that we are forgetting to look at the forest. Now I can hear, even in this cave, how the Christmas bells are ringing."

The words were barely uttered when they all sprang up and rushed out. But in the forest it was still dark night and bleak winter. The only thing they marked was a distant clang borne on a light south wind.

When the bells had been ringing a few moments, a sudden illumination penetrated the forest; the next moment it was dark again, and then light came back. It pushed its way forward between the stark trees, like a shimmering mist. The darkness merged into a faint daybreak. Then Abbot Hans saw that the snow had vanished from the ground, as if someone had removed a carpet, and the earth

began to take on a green covering. The moss-tufts thickened and raised themselves, and the spring blossoms shot upward their swelling buds, which already had a touch of color.

Again it grew hazy; but almost immediately there came a new wave of light. Then the leaves of the trees burst into bloom, crossbeaks hopped from branch to branch, and the woodpeckers hammered on the limbs until the splinters fairly flew around them. A flock of starlings from up country lighted in a fir top to rest.

When the next warm wind came along, the blueberries ripened and the baby squirrels began playing on the branches of the trees.

The next light wave that came rushing in brought with it the scent of newly ploughed acres. Pine and spruce trees were so thickly clothed with red cones that they shone like

crimson mantles and forest flowers covered the ground till it was all red, blue, and yellow.

Abbot Hans bent down to the earth and broke off a wild strawberry blossom, and, as he straightened up, the berry ripened in his hand.

The mother fox came out of her lair with a big litter of black-legged young. She went up to Robber Mother and scratched at her skirt, and Robber Mother bent down to her and praised her young.

Robber Mother's youngsters let out perfect shrieks of delight. They stuffed themselves with wild strawberries that hung on the bushes. One of them played with a litter of young hares; another ran a race with some young crows, which had hopped from their nest before they were really ready.

Robber Father was standing out on a marsh eating raspberries. When he glanced up, a big black bear stood beside him. Robber Father broke off a twig and struck the bear on the nose. "Keep to your own ground, you!" he said; "this is my turf." The huge bear turned around and lumbered off in another direction.

Then all the flowers whose seeds had been brought from foreign lands began to blossom. The loveliest roses climbed up the mountain wall in a race with the blackberry vines, and from the forest meadow sprang flowers as large as human faces.

Abbot Hans thought of the flower he was to pluck for Bishop Absalon; but each new flower that appeared was more beautiful than the others, and he wanted to choose the most beautiful of all.

Then Abbot Hans marked how all grew still; the birds hushed their songs, the flowers ceased growing, and the young foxes played no more. From far in the distance faint harp tones were heard, and celestial song, like a soft murmur, reached him.

He clasped his hands and dropped to his knees. His face was radiant with bliss.

But beside Abbot Hans stood the lay brother who had accompanied him. In his mind there were dark thoughts. "This

115

cannot be a true miracle," he thought, "since it is revealed to malefactors. This does not come from God, but is sent hither by Satan. It is the Evil One's power that is tempting us and compelling us to see that which has no real existence."

The angel throng was so near now that Abbot Hans saw their bright forms through the forest branches. The lay brother saw them, too; but back of all this wondrous beauty he saw only some dread evil.

All the while the birds had been circling around the head of Abbot Hans, and they let him take them in his hands. But all the animals were afraid of the lay brother; no bird perched on his shoulder, no snake played at his feet. Then there came a little forest dove. When she marked that the angels were

nearing, she plucked up courage and flew down on the lay brother's shoulder and laid her head against his cheek.

Then it appeared to him as if sorcery were come right upon him, to tempt and corrupt him. He struck with his hand at the forest dove and cried in such a loud voice that it rang throughout the forest, "Go thou back to hell, whence thou are come!"

Just then the angels were so near that Abbot Hans felt the feathery touch of their great wings, and he bowed down to earth in reverent greeting.

But when the lay brother's words sounded, their song was hushed and the holy guests turned in flight. At the same time the light and the mild warmth vanished in unspeakable terror for the darkness and cold in a human heart.

The Legend of the Christmas Rose

Darkness sank over the earth, like a coverlet; frost came, all the growths shriveled up; the animals and birds hastened away; the leaves dropped from the trees, rustling like rain.

Abbot Hans felt how his heart, which had but lately swelled with bliss, was now contracting with insufferable agony. "I can never outlive this," thought he, "that the angels from heaven had been so close to me and were driven away; that they wanted to sing Christmas carols for me and were driven to flight."

Then he remembered the flower he had promised Bishop Absalon, and at the last moment he fumbled among the

leaves and moss to try and find a blossom. But he sensed how the ground under his fingers froze and how the white snow came gliding over the ground. Then his heart caused him even greater anguish. He could not rise, but fell prostrate on the ground and lay there.

When the robber folk and the lay brother had groped their way back to the cave, they missed Abbot Hans. They took brands with them and went out to search for him. The found him dead upon the coverlet of snow.

When Abbot Hans had been carried down to Övid, those who took charge of the dead saw that he held his right hand locked tight around something which he must have grasped at the moment of death. When they finally got his hand open, they found that the

117

thing which he had held in such an iron grip was a pair of white root bulbs, which he had torn from among the moss and leaves.

When the lay brother who had accompanied Abbot Hans saw the bulbs, he took them and planted them in Abbot Hans' herb garden.

He guarded them the whole year to see if any flower would spring from them. But in vain he waited through the spring, the summer, and the autumn. Finally, when winter had set in and all the leaves and the flowers were dead, he ceased caring for them.

But when Christmas Eve came again, he was so strongly reminded of Abbot Hans that he wandered out into the garden to think of him. And look! as he came to the spot where he had planted the bare root bulbs, he saw that from them

had sprung flourishing green stalks, which bore beautiful flowers with silver white leaves.

He called out all the monks at Övid, and when they saw that this plant bloomed on Christmas Eve, when all the other growths were as if dead, they understood that this flower had in truth been plucked by Abbot Hans from the Christmas garden in Göinge forest. Then the lay brother asked the monks if he might take a few blossoms to Bishop Absalon.

When Bishop Absalon beheld the flowers, which had spring from

the earth in darkest winter, he turned as pale as if he had met a ghost. He sat in silence a moment; thereupon he said, "Abbot Hans has faithfully kept his word and I shall also keep mine."

He handed the letter of ransom to the lay brother, who departed at once for the Robbers' Cave. When he stepped in there on Christmas Day, the robber came toward him with axe uplifted. "I'd like to hack you monks into bits, as many as you are!" said he. "It must be your fault that Göinge forest did not last night dress itself in Christmas bloom."

"The fault is mine alone," said the lay brother, "and I will gladly die for it; but first I must deliver a message from Abbot Hans." And he drew forth the Bishop's letter and told the man that he was free.

Robber Father stood there pale and speechless, but Robber Mother said in his name, "Abbot Hans has indeed kept his word, and Robber Father will keep his."

When the robber and his wife left the cave, the lay brother moved in and lived all alone in the forest, in constant meditation and prayer that his hard-heartedness might be forgiven him.

But Göinge forest never again celebrated the hour of our Savior's birth; and of all its glory, there lives today only the plant which Abbot Hans had plucked. It has been named CHRISTMAS ROSE. And each year at Christmastide she sends forth from the earth her green stalks and white blossoms, as if she never could forget that she had once grown in the great Christmas garden at Göinge forest.

❄

New England Eggnog

This is, of course, the traditional Christmas party punch. Here, with the ice cream thrown in, we suggest serving it as an after-dinner drink.

4 eggs, separated

$1/4$ cup sugar

$1/2$ cup bourbon

$1/4$ cup dark rum

1 quart French vanilla ice cream, softened

1 cup whole milk

1 cup heavy cream

Nutmeg

1. Beat the egg yolks and the sugar until they are a mellow creamy yellow. Stir in the liquor, the soft ice cream, and the milk. Put the mixture in the freezer.

2. When ready to serve, whip the heavy cream and the egg whites. Fold into the mixture, thin with more milk if necessary, spoon into cups, and sprinkle with nutmeg.

Serves 8 to 10

Apple Cider with Cinnamon Sticks

*T**his is the perfect thing to serve to chilled carolers or the kids as they come in from sledding.*

1 quart (8 cups) of apple cider (or apple juice)

Peel from 1/2 orange

1 1-inch peeled and sliced piece of fresh ginger

1 teaspoon whole allspice

6 cinnamon sticks

Additional cinnamon sticks, one per cup (kids love to try to use these as straws!)

1. Put the apple juice or cider in a large saucepan over the lowest heat.

2. Wrap up the remaining ingredients in a big piece of cheesecloth and put it into the pot, or put them in a strainer that hooks over the pot. Simmer at the lowest heat for 4 to 5 hours.

3. Throw away the spices, pour the cider into mugs, and add a cinnamon stick.

Serves 8

The Story of the Goblins Who Stole a Sexton

Charles Dickens

In an old abbey town, down in this part of the country, a long, long while ago—so long, that the story must be a true one, because our great grandfathers implicitly believed it—there officiated as sexton and grave-digger in the churchyard, one Gabriel Grub. It by no means follows that because a man is a sexton, and constantly surrounded by the emblems of mortality, therefore he should be a morose and melancholy man; your undertakers are the merriest fellows in the world; and I once had the honour of being on intimate terms with a mute, who in private life, and off duty, was as comical and jocose a little fellow as ever chirped out a devil-may-care song, without a hitch in his memory, or drained off the contents of a good stiff glass without stopping for breath. But, notwithstanding these precedents to the contrary, Gabriel Grub was an ill-conditioned, cross-grained, surly fellow—a morose and lonely man, who consorted with nobody but himself, and an old wicker bottle which fitted into his large deep waistcoat pocket—and who eyed each merry face, as it passed him by, with such a deep scowl of malice and ill-humour, as it was difficult to meet, without feeling something the worse for.

"A little before twilight, one Christmas eve, Gabriel shouldered his spade, lighted his lantern, and betook himself towards the old churchyard; for he had got a grave to finish by next morning, and, feeling very low, he thought it might raise his spirits, perhaps, if he went on with his work at once. As he went his way, up the ancient street, he saw the cheerful light of the blazing fires gleam through the old casements, and heard the loud laugh and the cheerful shouts of those who were assembled around them; he marked the bustling preparations for next day's cheer, and smelt the numerous savoury odours consequent thereupon, as they steamed up from the kitchen windows in clouds. All this was gall and wormwood to the heart of Gabriel Grub; and when groups of children bounded out of the houses, tripped across the road, and were met, before they could knock at the opposite door, by half a dozen curly-headed little rascals who crowded round them as they flocked up-stairs to spend the evening in their Christmas games, Gabriel smiled grimly, and clutched the handle of his spade with a firmer grasp, as he thought of measles, scarlet-fever, thrush, whooping-cough, and a good many other sources of consolation besides.

"In this happy frame of mind, Gabriel strode along: returning a short, sullen growl to the good-humoured greetings of such of his neighbours as now and then passed him: until he turned into the dark lane which led to the churchyard. Now, Gabriel had been looking forward to reaching the dark lane, because it was, generally speaking, a nice, gloomy, mournful place, into which the towns-people did not much care to go, except in broad daylight, and when the sun was shining; consequently, he was not a little indignant to hear a young urchin roaring out some jolly song about a merry Christmas, in this very sanctuary, which had been called Coffin Lane ever since the days of the old abbey, and the time of the shaven-headed monks. As Gabriel walked on, and the voice drew nearer, he found it proceeded from a small boy, who was hurrying along, to join one of the little parties in the old street, and who, partly to keep himself company, and partly to prepare himself for the occasion, was shouting out the song at the highest pitch of his lungs. So Gabriel waited until the boy came up, and then dodged him into a corner, and rapped him over the head with his lantern five or six times, to teach him to modulate his voice. And as the boy hurried away with his hand to his head, singing quite a different sort of tune, Gabriel Grub chuckled very heartily to himself, and entered the churchyard: locking the gate behind him.

"He took off his coat, put down his lantern, and getting into the unfinished grave, worked at it for

an hour or so, with right good will. But the earth was hardened with the frost, and it was no very easy matter to break it up, and shovel it out; and although there was a moon, it was a very young one, and shed little light upon the grave, which was in the shadow of the church. At any other time, these obstacles would have made Gabriel Grub very moody and miserable, but he was so well pleased with having stopped the small boy's singing, that he took little heed of the scanty progress he had made, and looked down into the grave, when he had finished work for the night, with grim satisfaction: murmuring as he gathered up his things:

Brave lodgings for one, brave lodgings for one,

A few feet of cold earth, when life is done;
A stone at the head, a stone at the feet,
A rich, juicy meal for the worms to eat;
Rank grass overhead, and damp clay around,
Brave lodgings for one, these, in holy ground!

"'Ho! ho!' laughed Gabriel Grub, as he sat himself down on a flat tombstone which was a favourite resting-place of his; and drew forth his wicker bottle. 'A coffin at Christmas! A Christmas Box. Ho! ho! ho!'

"'Ho! ho! ho!' repeated a voice which sounded close behind him.

"Gabriel paused in some alarm, in the act of raising the wicker bottle to his lips; and looked round. The bottom of the oldest grave about him, was not more still and quiet, than the churchyard in the pale moonlight. The cold hoarfrost

127

glistened on the tombstones, and sparkled like rows of gems, among the stone carvings of the old church. The snow lay hard and crisp upon the ground; and spread over the thickly strewn mounds of earth so white and smooth a cover that it seemed as if corpses lay there, hidden only by their winding sheets. Not the faintest rustle broke the profound tranquility of the solemn scene. Sound itself appeared to be frozen up, all was so cold and still.

"'It was the echoes,' said Gabriel Grub, raising the bottle to his lips again.

"'It was *not*,' said a deep voice.

"Gabriel started up, and stood rooted to the spot with astonishment and terror; for his eyes rested on a form that made his blood run cold.

"Seated on an upright tombstone, close to him, was a strange unearthly figure, whom Gabriel felt at once, was no being of this world. His long fantastic legs which might have reached the ground, were cocked up, and crossed after a quaint, fantastic fashion; his sinewy arms were bare; and his hands rested on his knees. On his short round body, he wore a close covering, ornamented with small slashes; a short cloak dangled at his back; the collar was cut into curious peaks, which served the goblin in lieu of ruff or neckerchief; and his shoes curled up at his toes into long points. On his head, he wore a broad-brimmed sugar-loaf hat, garnished with a single feather. The hat was covered with the white frost; and the goblin looked as if he had sat on the same tombstone very comfortably, for two or three hundred years. He was sitting perfectly still; his tongue was put out, as if in derision; and he was grinning at Gabriel Grub with such a grin as only a goblin could call up.

"'It was not the echoes,' said the goblin.

"Gabriel Grub was paralysed, and could make no reply.

"'What do you do here on Christmas eve?' said the goblin sternly.

"'I came to dig a grave, sir,' stammered Gabriel Grub.

"'What man wanders among graves and churchyards on such a night as this?' cried the goblin.

"'Gabriel Grub! Gabriel Grub!' screamed a wild chorus of voices that seemed to fill the churchyard. Gabriel looked fearfully round—nothing was to be seen.

"'What have you got in that bottle?' said the goblin.

"'Hollands, sir,' replied the sexton, trembling more than ever; for he had bought it of the smugglers, and he thought that perhaps his questioner might be in the excise department of the goblins.

"'Who drinks Hollands alone, and in a churchyard, on such a night as this?' said the goblin.

"'Gabriel Grub! Gabriel Grub!' exclaimed the wild voices again.

"The goblin leered maliciously at the terrified sexton, and then raising his voice, exclaimed:

"'And who, then, is our fair and lawful price?'

"To this inquiry the invisible chorus replied, in a strain that sounded like the voices of many choristers singing to the mighty swell of the old church organ—a strain that seemed borne to the sexton's ears upon a wild wind, and to die away as it passed onward; but the burden of the reply was still the same, 'Gabriel Grub! Gabriel Grub!'

"The goblin grinned a broader grin than before, as he said, 'Well, Gabriel, what do you say to this?'

"The sexton gasped for breath.

"'What do you think of this, Gabriel?' said the goblin, kicking up his feet in the air on either side of the tombstone, and looking at the turned-up points with as much complacency as if he had been contemplating the most fashionable pair of Wellingtons in all Bond Street.

"'It's—it's—very curious, sir,' replied the sexton, half dead with fright; 'very curious, and very pretty, but I think I'll go back and finish my work, sir, if you please.'

"'Work!' said the goblin, 'what work?'

"'The grave, sir; making the grave,' stammered the sexton.

"'Oh, the grave, eh?' said the goblin; 'who makes graves at a time when all other men are merry, and takes a pleasure in it?'

"Again the mysterious voices replied, "Gabriel Grub! Gabriel Grub!'

"'I'm afraid my friends want you, Gabriel,' said the goblin, thrusting his tongue further into his cheek than ever—and a most astonishing tongue it was—I'm afraid my friends want you, Gabriel,' said the goblin.

"'Under favour, sir,' replied the horror-stricken sexton, 'I don't think they can, sir; they don't know me, sir; I don't think the gentlemen have ever seen me, sir.'

"'Oh yes, they have,' replied the goblin; 'we know the man with the sulky face and grim scowl, that came down the street to-night, throwing his evil looks at the children, and grasping his burying spade the tighter. We know the man who struck the boy in the envious malice of his heart, because the boy could be merry, and he could not. We know him, we know him.'

"Here, the goblin gave a loud shrill laugh, which the echoes returned twenty-fold: and throwing his legs up in the air, stood upon his head, or rather upon the very point of his sugar-loaf hat, on the narrow edge of the tombstone: whence he threw a somerset with extraordinary agility, right to the sexton's feet, at which he planted himself in the attitude in which tailors generally sit upon the shopboard.

"'I—I—am afraid I must leave you, sir,' said the sexton, making an effort to move.

"'Leave us!' said the goblin, 'Gabriel Grub going to leave us. Ho! ho! ho!'

"As the goblin laughed, the sexton observed, for one instant, a brilliant illumination within the windows of the church, as if the whole building were lighted up; it disappeared, the organ pealed forth a lively air, and whole troops of goblins, the very counterpart of the first one, poured into the churchyard, and began playing at leap-frog with the tombstones: never stopping for an instant to take breath, but 'overing' the highest among them, one after the other, with the most marvellous dexterity. The first goblin was a most astonishing leaper, and none of the others could come near him; even in the extremity of his terror the sexton could not help observing, that while his friends were content

to leap over the common-sized gravestones, the first one took the family vaults, iron railings and all, with as much ease as if they had been so many street posts. At last the game reached to a most exciting pitch; the organ played quicker and quicker; and the goblins leaped faster and faster: coiling themselves up, rolling head over heels upon the ground, and bounding over the tombstones like foot-balls. The sexton's brain whirled round with the rapidity of the motion he beheld, and his legs reeled beneath him, as the spirits flew before his eyes: when the goblin king, suddenly darting towards him, laid his hand upon his collar, and sank with him through the earth.

"When Gabriel Grub had had time to fetch his breath, which the rapidity of his descent had for the moment taken away, he found himself in what appeared to be a large cavern, surrounded on all sides by crowds of goblins, ugly and grim; in the centre of the room, on an elevated seat, was stationed his friend of the churchyard; and close beside him stood Gabriel Grub himself, without power of motion.

"'Cold to-night,' said the king of goblins, 'very cold. A glass of something warm, here!'

"At this command, half a dozen officious goblins, with a perpetual smile upon their faces, whom Gabriel Grub imagined to be courtiers, on that account, hastily disappeared, and presently returned with a goblet of liquid fire, which they presented to the king.

"'Ah!' cried the goblin, whose cheeks and throat were transparent, as he tossed down the flame, 'this warms one, indeed! Bring a bumper of the same for Mr. Grub.'

"It was in vain for the unfortunate sexton to protest that he was not in the habit of taking anything warm at night; one of the goblins held him while another poured the blazing liquid down his throat; the whole assembly screeched with laughter as he coughed and choked, and wiped away the tears which gushed plentifully from his eyes, after swallowing the burning draught.

"'And now,' said the king, fantastically poking the taper corner of his sugar-loaf hat into the sexton's eyes, and thereby occasioning him the most exquisite pain: 'And now, show the man of misery and gloom, a few of the pictures from our own great storehouse!'

"As the goblin said this, a thick cloud which obscured the remoter end of the cavern, rolled gradually away, and disclosed, apparently at a great distance, a small and scantily furnished, but neat and clean apartment. A crowd of little children were gathered round a bright fire, clinging to their mother's gown, and gambolling around her chair. The mother occasionally rose, and drew aside the window-curtain, as if to look for some expected object; a frugal meal was ready spread upon the table, and an elbow chair was placed near the fire. A knock was heard at the door; the mother opened it, and the children crowded round her, and clapped their hands for joy, as their father entered. He was wet and weary, and shook the snow from his

135

garments, as the children crowded round him, and seizing his cloak, hat, stick, and gloves, with busy zeal, ran with them from the room. Then, as he sat down to his meal before the fire, the children climbed about his knee, and the mother sat by his side, and all seemed happiness and comfort.

"But a change came upon the view, almost imperceptibly. The scene was altered to a small bedroom, where the fairest and youngest child lay dying; the roses had fled from his cheek, and the light from the eye; and even as the sexton looked upon him with an interest he had never felt or known before, he died. His young brothers and sisters crowded round his little bed, and seized his tiny hand, so cold and heavy; but they shrunk back from its touch, and looked with awe on his infant face; for

calm and tranquil as it was and sleeping in rest and peace as the beautiful child seemed to be, they saw that he was dead, and they knew that he was an Angel looking down upon, and blessing them, from a bright and happy Heaven.

"Again the light cloud passed across the picture, and again the subject changed. The father and mother were old and helpless now, and the number of those about them was diminished more than half; but content and cheerfulness sat on every face, and beamed in every eye, as they crowded round the fireside, and told and listened to old stories of earlier and bygone days. Slowly and peacefully, the father sank into the grave, and, soon after, the sharer of all his cares and troubles followed him to a place of rest. The few, who yet survived them, knelt by their tomb,

and watered the green turf which covered it, with their tears; then rose, and turned away: sadly and mournfully, but not with bitter cries, or despairing lamentations, for they knew that they should one day meet again; and once more they mixed with the busy world, and their content and cheerfulness were restored. The cloud settled upon the picture, and concealed it from the sexton's view.

"'What do you think of *that*?' said the goblin, turning his large face towards Gabriel Grub.

"Gabriel murmured out something about its being very pretty, and looked somewhat ashamed, as the goblin bent his fiery eyes upon him.

"'*You* a miserable man!' said the goblin, in a tone of excessive contempt. 'You!' He appeared disposed to add more, but

indignation choked his utterance, so he lifted up one of his very pliable legs, and flourishing it above his head a little, to insure his aim, administered a good sound kick to Gabriel Grub; immediately after which, all the goblins in waiting crowded round the wretched sexton, and kicked him without mercy: according to the established and invariable custom of courtiers upon earth, who kick whom royalty kicks, and hug whom royalty hugs.

"'Show him some more!' said the king of the goblins.

"At these words, the cloud was dispelled, and a rich and beautiful landscape was disclosed to view— there is just such another, to this day, within half a mile of the old abbey town. The sun shone from out the clear blue sky, the water sparkled beneath its rays, and the trees looked greener, and the flowers more gay, beneath his cheering influence. The water rippled on, with a pleasant sound; the trees rustled in the light wind that murmured among their leaves; the birds sang upon the boughs; and the lark carolled on high her welcome to the morning. Yes, it was morning; the bright, balmy morning of summer; the minutest leaf, the smallest blade of grass, was instinct with life. The ant crept forth to her daily toil, the butterfly fluttered and basked in the warm rays of the sun; myriads of insects spread their transparent wings, and revelled in their brief but happy existence. Man walked forth, elated with the scene; and all was brightness and splendour.

"'*You* a miserable man!' said the king of the goblins, in a more contemptuous tone than before. And again the king of the goblins gave his leg a flourish; again it descended on the shoulders of the sexton; and again the attendant goblins imitated the example of their chief.

"Many a time the cloud went and came, and many a lesson it taught to Gabriel Grub, who, although his shoulders smarted with pain from the frequent applications of the goblins' feet, looked on with an interest that nothing could diminish. He saw that men who worked hard, and earned their scanty bread with lives of labour, were cheerful and happy; and that to the most ignorant, the sweet face of nature was a never-failing source of cheerfulness and joy. He saw those who had been

delicately nurtured, and tenderly brought up, cheerful under privations, and superior to suffering that would have crushed many of a rougher grain, because they bore within their own bosoms the materials of happiness, content-ment, and peace. He saw that women, the tenderest and most fragile of all God's creatures, were the oftenest superior to sorrow, adversity, and distress; and he saw that it was because they bore, in their own hearts, an inexhaustible well-spring of affection and devotion. Above all, he saw that men like himself, who snarled at the mirth and cheerfulness of others, were the foulest weeds on the fair surface of the earth; and setting all the good of the world against the evil, he came to the conclusion that it was a very decent and respectable sort of world after all. No sooner had he formed it, than the cloud which closed over the last picture, seemed to settle on his senses, and lull him to repose. One by one, the goblins faded from his sight; and as the last one disappeared, he sunk to sleep.

"The day had broken when Gabriel Grub awoke, and found himself lying, at full length on the flat gravestone in the churchyard, with the wicker bottle lying empty by his side, and his coat, spade, and lantern, all well whitened by the last night's frost, scattered on the ground. The stone on which he had first seen the goblin seated stood bolt upright before him, and the grave at which he had worked, the night before, was not far off. At first, he began to doubt the reality of his adventures, but the acute pain in his shoulders when he attempted to rise assured him that the kicking of the goblins was certainly not ideal. He was staggered again by observing no traces of footsteps in the snow on which the goblins had played at leap-frog with the gravestones, but he speedily accounted for this circumstance when he remembered that, being spirits, they would leave no visible impression behind them. So, Gabriel Grub got on his feet as well as he could, for the pain in his back; and brushing the frost off his coat, put it on, and turned his face towards the town.

"But he was an altered man, and he could not bear the thought of returning to a place where his repentance would be scoffed at, and his reformation disbelieved. He hesitated for a few moments; and then turned away to wander where he might, and seek his bread elsewhere.

"The lantern, the spade, and the wicker bottle, were found, that day, in the churchyard. There were a great many speculations about the sexton's fate, at first, but it was speedily determined that he had been carried away by the goblins; and there were not wanting some very credible witnesses who had distinctly seen him whisked through the air on the back of a chestnut horse blind of one eye, with the hind-quarters of a lion, and the tail of a bear. At length all this was devoutly believed; and the new sexton used to exhibit to the curious, for a trifling emolument, a good-sized piece of the church weathercock which had been accidentally kicked off by the aforesaid horse in his aerial flight, and picked up by himself in the churchyard, a year or two afterwards.

"Unfortunately, these stories were somewhat disturbed by the unlooked-for re-appearance of Gabriel Grub himself, some ten years afterwards, a ragged, contented, rheumatic old man. He told his story to the clergyman, and also to the mayor; and in course of time it began to be received, as a matter of history, in which form it has continued down to this very day. The believers in the weathercock tale, having misplaced their confidence once, were not easily prevailed upon to part with it again, so they looked as wise as they could, shrugged their shoulders, touched their foreheads, and murmured something about Gabriel Grub having drunk all the Hollands, and then fallen asleep on the flat tombstone; and they affected to explain what he supposed he had witnessed in the goblin's cavern, by saying that he had seen the world, and grown wiser. But this opinion, which was by no means a popular one at any time, gradually died off; and be the matter how it may, as Gabriel Grub was afflicted with rheumatism to the end of his days, this story has at least one moral, if it teach no better one—and that is, that if a man turn sulky and drink by himself at Christmas time, he may

make up his mind to be not a bit the better for it: let the spirits be never so good, or let them be even as many degrees beyond proof, as those which Gabriel Grub saw in the goblin's cavern." ❄

Vermont Whiskey Cake

Baking doesn't get much easier or better than this. This cake is so simple and delicious that you will probably make it again and again throughout the year! You can use a bundt cake mold, a loaf pan, or make individual cakes using mini-bundt molds or cupcake pans.

CAKE:
1 box yellow cake mix
1 box instant vanilla pudding
1 cup water
1/2 cup salad oil
4 eggs

1. Preheat oven to 350°F.
2. Grease and flower bundt cake mold well.
3. Mix all ingredients together until smooth.
4. Pour into bundt cake mold and bake for 1 hour.

WHISKEY MIXTURE:
1/2 cup sugar
1/4 cup butter
1/2 cup whiskey

1. Melt whiskey mixture ingredients together in small pan.
2. Remove cake from oven after 1 hour. Spoon whiskey mixture over cake slowly, letting it sink in.
3. Return cake to 350°F oven and bake for another 5 minutes.
4. Cool and remove from pan.

Serves 8 to 10

Good King Wenceslas

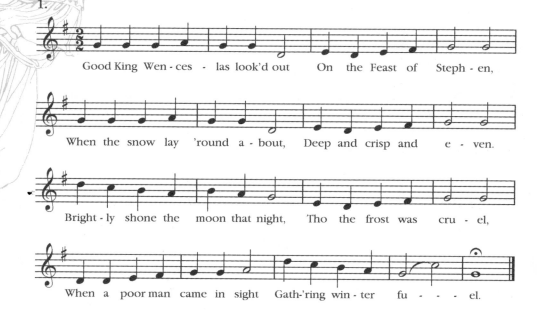

1.

Good King Wen - ces - las look'd out On the Feast of Steph - en,

When the snow lay 'round a - bout, Deep and crisp and e - ven.

Bright - ly shone the moon that night, Tho the frost was cru - el,

When a poor man came in sight Gath'ring win - ter fu - - - el.

2. "Hither, page and stand by me,
    If thou know'st it, telling,
    Yonder peasant, who is he?
    Where and what his dwelling?"
    "Sire, he lives a good league hence
    Underneath the mountain;
    Right against the forest fence,
    By saint Agnes fountain!"

3. "Bring me flesh, and bring me wine,
    Bring me pinelogs hither;
    Thou and I will see him dine
    When we bear them hither."
    Page and monarch forth they went,
    Forth they went together:
    Thro' the rude wind's wild lament
    And the bitter weather.

4. "Sire, the night is darker now,
    And the wind blows stronger;
    Fails my heart, I know not how,
    I can go no longer."
    "Mark my footsteps, my good page.
    Tread thou in them boldly,
    Thou shalt find the winter's rage
    Freeze thy blood less coldly!"

5. In his master's steps he trod,
    Where the snow lay dinted;
    Heat was in the very sod
    Which the saint had printed;
    Therefore, Christian men, be sure,
    Wealth or rank possessing,
    Ye who now will bless the poor,
    Shall yourselves find blessing.

Christmas Eve in the Blue Chamber

Jerome K. Jerome

I don't want to make you fellows nervous," began my uncle in a peculiarly impressive, not to say blood-curdling, tone of voice, "and if you would rather that I did not mention it, I won't; but, as a matter of fact, this very house, in which we are now sitting, is haunted."

"You don't say that!" exclaimed Mr. Coombes.

"What's the use of your saying I don't say it when I have just said it?" retorted my uncle somewhat annoyed. "You talk so foolishly. I tell you the house is haunted. Regularly on Christmas Eve the Blue Chamber" (they call the room next to the nursery the "Blue Chamber" at my uncle's) "is haunted by the ghost of a sinful man—a man who once killed a Christmas carol singer with a lump of coal."

"How did he do it?" asked Mr. Coombes, eagerly. "Was it difficult?"

"I do not know how he did it," replied my uncle; "he did not explain the process. The singer had taken up a position just inside the front gate, and was singing a ballad. It is presumed that, when he opened his mouth for B flat, the lump of coal was thrown by the sinful man from one of the windows, and that it went down the singer's throat and choked him."

"You want to be a good shot, but it is certainly worth trying," murmured Mr. Coombes thoughtfully.

"But that was not his only crime, alas!" added my uncle. "Prior to that he had killed a solo cornet player."

"No! Is that really a fact?" exclaimed Mr. Coombes.

"Of course it's a fact," answered my uncle testily. "At all events, as much a fact as you can expect to get in a case of this sort.

"The poor fellow, the cornet player, had been in the neighborhood barely a month. Old Mr. Bishop, who kept the 'Jolly Sand Boys' at the time, and from whom I had the story, said he had never known a more hard-working and energetic solo cornet player. He, the cornet player, only knew two tunes, but Mr. Bishop said that the man could not have played with more

vigor, or for more hours a day, if he had known forty. The two tunes he did play were 'Annie Laurie' and 'Home, Sweet Home'; and as regarded his performance of the former melody, Mr. Bishop said that a mere child could have told what it was meant for.

"This musician— this poor, friendless artist—used to come regularly and play in this street just opposite for two hours every evening. One evening he was seen, evidently in response to an invitation, going into this very house, *but was never seen coming out of it!*"

"Did the townsfolk try offering any reward for his recovery?" asked Mr. Coombes.

"Not a penny," replied my uncle.

"Another summer," continued my uncle, "a German band visited here, intending—so they announced on their arrival—to stay till the autumn.

"On the second day after their arrival, the whole company, as fine and healthy a body of men as one would wish to see, were invited to dinner by this sinful man, and, after spending the whole of the next twenty-four hours in bed, left the town a broken and dyspeptic crew; the parish doctor, who had attended them, giving it as his opinion that it was doubtful if they would, any of them, be fit to play an air again."

"You—you don't know the recipe, do you?" asked Mr. Coombes.

"Unfortunately I do not," replied my uncle; "but the chief ingredient was said to have been railway dining-room hash.

"I forget the man's other crimes," my uncle went on; "I used to know them all at one time, but my memory is not what it was. I do not, however, believe I am doing his memory an injustice in believing that he was not entirely unconnected with the death, and subsequent burial, of a gentleman who used to play the harp with his toes; and that neither was he altogether unresponsible for the lonely grave of an unknown stranger who had once visited the neighborhood, an Italian peasant lad, a performer upon the barrel-organ.

"Every Christmas Eve," said my

150

uncle, cleaving with low impressive tones the strange awed silence that, like a shadow, seemed to have slowly stolen into and settled down upon the room, "the ghost of this sinful man haunts the Blue Chamber, in this very house. There, from midnight until cock-crow, amid wild muffled shrieks and groans and mocking laughter and the ghostly sound of horrid blows, it does fierce phantom fight with the spirits of the solo cornet player and the murdered carol singer, assisted at intervals by the shades of the German band; while the ghost of the strangled harpist plays mad ghostly melodies with ghostly toes on the ghost of a broken harp."

Uncle said the Blue Chamber was comparatively useless as a sleeping apartment on Christmas Eve.

"Hark!" said my uncle, raising a warning hand toward the ceiling, while we held our breath, and listened: "Hark! I believe they are at it now—in the Blue Chamber!"

I rose up and said the *I* would sleep in the Blue Chamber.

"Never!" cried my uncle, springing up. "You shall not put yourself in this deadly peril. Besides, the bed is not made."

"Never mind the bed," I replied. "I have lived in furnished apartments for gentlemen, and have been accustomed to sleep on beds that have never been made from one year's end to the other. I am young, and have had a clear conscience now for a month. The spirits will not harm me. I may even do them some little good, and induce them to be quiet and go away. Besides, I should like to see the show."

They tried to dissuade me from what they termed my foolhardy enterprise, but I remained firm and claimed my privilege. I was "the guest." "The guest" always sleeps in the haunted chamber on Christmas Eve; it is his right.

They said that if I put it on that footing they had, of course, no answer, and they lighted a candle for me and followed me upstairs in a body.

Whether elevated by the feeling that I was doing a noble action or animated by a mere general consciousness of rectitude is not for me to say, but I went upstairs that night with remarkable buoyancy. It was as much as I could do to stop at the landing when I came to it; I felt I wanted to go on up to the roof. But, with the help of the banisters, I restrained by ambition, wished them all good-night and went in and shut the door.

Things began to go wrong with

me from the very first. The candle tumbled out of the candlestick before my hand was off the lock. It kept on tumbling out again; I never saw such a slippery candle. I gave up attempting to use the candlestick at last and carried the candle about in my hand, and even then it would not keep upright. So I got wild and threw it out the window, and undressed and went to bed in the dark.

I did not go to sleep; I did not feel sleepy at all; I lay on my back looking up at the ceiling and thinking of things. I wish I could remember some of the ideas that came to me as I lay there, because they were so amusing.

I had been lying like this for half an hour or so, and had forgotten all about the ghost, when, on casually casting my eyes round the room, I noticed for the first time a singularly contented-looking phantom sitting in the easy-chair by the fire smoking the ghost of a long clay pipe.

I fancied for the moment, as most people would under similar circumstances, that I must be dreaming. I sat up and rubbed by eyes. No! It was a ghost, clear enough. I could see the back of the chair through his body. He looked over toward me, took the shadowy pipe from his lips and nodded.

The most surprising part of the whole thing to me was that I did not feel in the least alarmed. If anything I was rather pleased to see him. It was company.

I said: "Good evening. It's been a cold day!"

He said he had not

noticed it himself, but dared say I was right.

We remained silent for a few seconds, and then, wishing to put it pleasantly, I said: "I believe I have the honor of addressing the ghost of the gentleman who had the accident with the carol singer?"

He smiled and said it was very good of me to remember it. One singer was not much to boast of, but still every little helped.

I was somewhat staggered at his answer. I had expected a groan of remorse. The ghost appeared, on the contrary, to be rather conceited over the business. I thought that as he had taken my reference to the singer so quietly perhaps he would not be offended if I questioned him about the organ grinder. I felt curious about that poor boy.

"Is it true," I asked, "that you had a hand in the death of that Italian peasant lad who came to the town with a barrel-organ that played nothing but Scotch airs?"

He quite fired up. "Had a hand in it!" he exclaimed indignantly. "Who has dared to pretend that he assisted me? I murdered the youth myself. Nobody helped me. Alone I did it. Show me the man who says I didn't."

I calmed him. I assured him that I had never, in my own mind, doubted that he was the real and only assassin, and I went on and asked him what he had done with the body of the cornet player he had killed.

He said: "To which one may you be alluding?

"Oh, were there any more then?" I inquired.

He smiled and gave a little cough. He said he did not like to appear to be boasting, but that,

155

counting trombones, there were seven.

"Dear me!" I replied, "you must have had quite a busy time of it, one way and another."

He said that perhaps he ought not to be the one to say so; but that really, speaking of ordinary middle-class society, he thought there were few ghosts who could look back upon a life of more sustained usefulness.

He puffed away in silence for a few seconds while I sat watching him. I had never seen a ghost smoking a pipe before, that I could remember, and it interested me.

I asked him what tobacco he used, and he replied: "The ghost of cut cavendish as a rule."

He explained that the ghost of all the tobacco that a man smoked in life belong to him when he became dead. He said he himself had smoked a good deal of cut cavendish when he was alive, so that he was well supplied with the ghost of it now.

I thought I would join him in a pipe, and he said, "Do, old man"; and I reached over and got out the necessary paraphernalia from my coat pocket and lit up.

We grew quite chummy after that, and he told me all his crimes. He said he had lived next door once to a young lady who was learning to play the guitar, while a gentleman who practiced on the bass-viol lived opposite. And he, with fiendish cunning, had introduced these two unsuspecting young people to one another, and had persuaded them to elope with each other against their parents' wishes, and take their musical instruments with them; and they had done so, and before the honeymoon was over, *she* had broken his head with the bass-viol, and *he* had tried to cram the guitar down her throat, and had injured her for life.

My friend said he used to lure muffin-men into the passage and then stuff them with their own wares till they burst. He said he had quieted eighteen that way.

Young men and women who recited long and dreary poems at evening parties, and callow youths who walked about the streets late at night, playing concertinas, he used to get together and poison in batches of ten, so as to save expenses; and park orators and temperance lecturers he used to shut up six in a small room with a glass of water and a collection-box apiece, and let them talk each other to death.

It did one good to listen to him.

I asked him when he expected the other ghosts—the ghosts of the singer and the cornet player, and the German band that Uncle John had mentioned. He smiled, and said they would never come again, any of them.

I said, "Why, isn't it true, then, that they meet you here every Christmas Eve for a row?"

He replied that it was true. Every Christmas Eve, for twenty-five years, had he and they fought in that room; but they would never trouble him or anybody else again. One by one had he laid them out, spoiled and made them utterly useless for all haunting purposes. He had finished off the last German band ghost that very evening, just before I came upstairs, and had thrown what was left of it out through the slit between the window sashes. He said it would never be worth calling a ghost again.

"I suppose you will still come

157

yourself, as usual?" I said. "They would be sorry to miss you, I know."

"Oh, I don't know," he replied; "there's noshing much to come for now; unless," he added kindly, "*you* are going to be here. I'll come if you will sleep here next Christmas Eve."

"I have taken a liking to you," he continued; "you don't fly off, screeching, when you see a party, and your hair doesn't stand on end. You've no idea," he said, "how sick I am of seeing people's hair standing on end."

He said it irritated him.

Just then a slight noise reached us from the yard below, and he started and turned deathly black.

"You are ill," I cried, springing toward him; "tell me the best thing to do for you. Shall I drink some brandy, and give you the ghost of it?"

He remained silent, listening intently for a moment, and then he gave a sigh of relief, and the shade came back to his cheek.

"It's all right," he murmured; "I was afraid it was the cock."

"Oh, it's too early for that," I said. "Why, it's only the middle of the night."

"Oh, that doesn't make any difference to those cursed chickens," he replied bitterly. "They would just as soon crow in the middle of the night as at any other time—sooner, if they thought it would spoil a chap's evening out. I believe they do it on purpose."

He said a friend of his, the ghost of a man who had killed a tax collector, used to haunt a house in Long Acre, where they kept fowls in the cellar, and every time a policeman went by and flashed his searchlight down the grating, the old cock there would fancy it was the sun, and start crowing like mad, when, of course, the poor ghost had to dissolve, and it would, in consequence, get back home sometimes as early as one o'clock in the morning, furious because it had only been out for an hour.

I agreed that it seemed very unfair.

"Oh, it's an absurd arrangement altogether," he continued, quite angrily. "I can't imagine what our chief could have been thinking of when he made it. As I have said to him, over and over again, 'Have a fixed time, and let everybody stick to it—say four o'clock in summer, and six in winter. Then, one would know what one was about.'"

"How do you manage when there isn't any clock handy?" I inquired.

He was on the point of replying, when again he started and listened.

This time I distinctly heard Mr. Bowles' cock, next door, crow twice.

"There you are," he said, rising and reaching for his hat; "that's the sort of thing we have to put up with. What *is* the time?"

I looked at my watch, and found it was half-past three.

"I thought as much," he muttered. "I'll wring that blessed bird's neck if I get hold of it." And he prepared to go.

"If you can wait half a minute," I said, getting out of bed, "I'll go a bit of the way with you."

"It's very good of you," he replied, pausing, "but it seems unkind to drag you out."

"Not at all," I replied; "I shall like a walk." And I partially dressed myself, and took my umbrella; and he put his arm through mine, and we went out together, the best of friends. ❄

159

Mistletoe

Walter de la Mare

Sitting under the mistletoe
(Pale-green, fairy mistletoe),
One last candle burning low,
All the sleepy dancers gone,
Just one candle burning on,
Shadows lurking everywhere:
Some one came, and kissed me there.

Tired I was; my head would go
Nodding under the mistletoe
(Pale-green, fairy mistletoe),
No footsteps came, no voice, but only,
Just as I sat there, sleepy, lonely,
Stooped in the still and shadowy air
Lips unseen—and kissed me there.

Classic Sugar Cookies

These can be enhanced with lemon or orange zest, but even plain, they are the perfect holiday treat.

1 cup butter (2 sticks), at room
    temperature
1 cup sugar
2 eggs
1 teaspoon vanilla extract
3 cups flour

1. Cream the butter and sugar. Beat in the eggs and add the vanilla. Add the flour and mix well. Refrigerate for at least 2 hours.

2. Preheat the oven to 375°F and line baking sheets with parchment paper.

3. Roll the dough out on a lightly floured surface (marble or wood) and cut with a cookie cutter. Transfer the cookies with a spatula to cookie sheets. If you are going to decorate without icing, decorate with sprinkles and move the sheets into the oven. Bake for approximately 10 minutes. When the cookies are beginning to brown, remove them from the oven and slide the parchment off the baking sheet. When the cookies have cooled a bit, slide them off the parchment. Cool the cookie sheets before using them again. If you have baked the cookies without decorations, wait until they are completely cool before icing. (See Snow Icing recipe on page 281 and Icing Hints on page 351.)

3 to 5 dozen cookies
depending on size and thickness

Christmas
This Year

Booth Tarkington

Something more than a dozen years ago, at Princeton, I heard from one of the "Art Professors" that a painting by Mainardi, a fine example from the Florentine Renaissance of the high period, could be bought in New York for far less than its worth. The great Depression was then upon us; the picture had been put through an auction sale and a dealer had bid it in for a fiftieth of what had once been paid for it.

I went to his galleries; he brought out the painting and I stood puzzled before it. The central figure was that of the blonde Virgin enthroned and holding the Christ child upon her lap. That was plain enough; but who were the two tall saints flanking the throne? One, holding a book, was a woman, probably identifiable as Ste. Justina; the other one was the problem—a long, thin, elderly man, bearded, ecclesiastically robed, red-gloved and carrying four loaves of bread in token of what function I couldn't guess.

One thing was certain: this ancient gentleman was

immeasurably compassionate. That was markedly his expression. A deep world sadness underlay the look of pity; he was visibly a person who suffered less his own anguish and more that of others. You saw at once that he was profoundly sorry for all of humankind.

When I had the painting on my own wall at home, I found that a gentle melancholy pervaded the room and the old saint seemed to add a wistfulness. "Don't you really wish to know who I am?" he inquired to me whenever I looked his way.

I did indeed wish to know him and to understand his sorrow, which was one of the kind we call "haunting"—all the more so because it was universal. Of all the saints, he was the one who most mourned over the miseries of this tangled world. We got out our books, wrote

to iconographical experts—and lo! we had our man. The sad old saint is—Santa Claus!

He is St. Nicholas of Bari and his four loaves of bread signify his giving, his generosity. In time, as the legend grew and changed, the most jocund and hearty of all symbolic figures emerged from this acutely sad and grieving one. St. Nicholas of Bari became "Old Saint Nick," "Kriss-kringle" (a most twisted

alliterative) and Santa Claus.

He, the troubled and unhappy, now comes laughing down the chimney, fat and merry, to be the jovial inspiration of our jolliest season of the year. We say that time changed him, made this metamorphosis; but it was we— "we-the-people"—who did it. Time only let us forget that St. Nicholas was a sorrowful man.

Mainardi put a date on the painting. It is clear and neat upon a step of the Virgin's throne—1507. In the long march of mankind, the four hundred and thirty-eight years that have elapsed since the Tuscan painter finished his picture is but a breath. St. Nicholas as we know him now, our jolly, shouting friend, a frolic for the children, may become the saddest of all the saints again, someday. What made us brighten him into Santa Claus was our knowledge that the world was growing kinder than it was in 1507.

St. Nicholas of Bari knew only a cruel world. Christmas of this year needs the transfigured image of him—the jolly one who is merry because the world is wise—and kind.

A Visit from St. Nicholas

Clement Clarke Moore

'Twas the night before Christmas, when all through the house
Not a creature was stirring, not even a mouse.
The stockings were hung by the chimney with care,
In hopes that St. Nicholas soon would be there.
The children were nestled all snug in their beds,
While visions of sugar-plums danced in their heads;
And mamma in her kerchief, and I in my cap,
Had just settled our brains for a long winter's nap—
When out on the lawn there arose such a clatter
I sprang from my bed to see what was the matter.
Away to the window I flew like a flash,
Tore open the shutter, and threw up the sash.
The moon on the breast of the new-fallen snow

Gave a lustre of midday to objects below;
When what to my wondering eye should appear
But a miniature sleigh and eight tiny reindeer,
With a little old driver, so lively and quick,
I knew in a moment it must be St. Nick!
More rapid than eagles his coursers they came,
And he whistled and shouted and called them by name.
"Now, Dasher! now, Dancer! now, Prancer and Vixen!
On, Comet! on, Cupid! on, Donder and Blitzen!—
To the top of the porch, to the top of the wall,
Now, dash away, dash away, dash away all!"
As dry leaves that before the wild hurricane fly,
When they meet with an obstacle mount to the sky,
So, up to the housetop the coursers they flew,
With a sleigh full of toys—and St. Nicholas, too.
And then, in a twinkling, I heard on the roof

The prancing and pawing of each little hoof.
As I drew in my head and was turning around,
Down the chimney St. Nicholas came with a bound:
He was dressed all in fur from his head to his foot,
And his clothes were all tarnished with ashes and soot:
A bundle of toys he had flung on his back,
And he looked like a peddler just opening his pack.
His eyes, how they twinkled! his dimples, how merry!
His cheeks were like roses, his nose like a cherry;
His droll little mouth was drawn up like a bow,
And the beard on his chin was as white as the snow.
The stump of a pipe he held tight in his teeth,
And the smoke, it encircled his head like a wreath.
He had a broad face and a little round belly
That shook, when he laughed, like a bowl full of jelly.
He was chubby and plump—a right jolly old elf:

And I laughed when I saw him, in spite of myself;
A wink of his eye, and a twist of his head,
Soon gave me to know I had nothing to dread.
He spoke not a word, but went straight to his work,
And filled all the stockings: then turned with a jerk,
And laying his finger aside of his nose,
And giving a nod, up the chimney he rose.
He sprang to his sleigh, to his team gave a whistle,
And away they all flew like the down of a thistle.
But I heard him exclaim, ere they drove out of sight,
"Happy Christmas to all, and to all a good-night!"

175

Dear Editor:

I am 8 years old. Some of
my friends say there is no
Santa Claus. Papa says
"If you see it in The Sun
it's so." Please tell me
the truth; is there a
Santa Claus?

Virginia O'Hanlon

Yes, Virginia, There Is a Santa Claus

Francis P. Church

Virginia, your little friends are wrong. They have been affected by the skepticism of a skeptical age. They do not believe except they see. They think that nothing can be which is not comprehensible by their little minds. All minds, Virginia, whether they be men's or children's, are little. In this great universe of ours man is a mere insect, an ant, in his intellect, as compared with the boundless world about him, as measured by the intelligence capable of grasping the whole of truth and knowledge.

Yes, Virginia, there is a Santa Claus. He exists as certainly as love and generosity and devotion exist, and you know that they abound and give to your life its highest beauty and joy. Alas! how dreary would be the world if there were no Santa Claus! It would be as dreary as if there were no Virginias. There would be no childlike faith then, no poetry, no romance to make tolerable this existence. We should have no enjoyment, except in sense and sight. The eternal light with which childhood fills the world would be extinguished.

Not believe in Santa Claus! You might as well not believe in fairies! You might get your papa to hire men to watch in all the chimneys on Christmas Eve to catch Santa Claus, but even if they did not see Santa Claus coming down, what would that prove? Nobody sees Santa Claus, but that is no sign that there is no Santa Claus. The most real things in the world are those that neither children nor men can see.

No Santa Claus! Thank God, he lives, and he lives forever. A thousand years from now, Virginia, nay, ten times ten thousand years from now, he will continue to make glad the heart of childhood.

—*The New York Sun*,
September 21, 1897

Great Refrigerator Cookies

*T*his is an extraordinary recipe because you can make so
many different cookies from the dough. You can keep the
dough in the refrigerator for up to two weeks and in the freezer
for up to three months.

2 cups unsalted butter (4 sticks), at
   room temperature

$1/2$ cup sugar

2 teaspoons vanilla extract

$2^1/2$ cups all purpose white flour

1 or 2 tablespoons cocoa

1. Mix the butter and sugar until creamy and fluffy. Add the vanilla and then mix in the flour. Mold the dough into a ball with lightly floured hands.

2. Divide the dough in half. Add the cocoa to one half. Wrap the 2 halves separately in plastic wrap or waxed paper and refrigerate for at least 2 hours. After the dough is chilled, remove it from the refrigerator and choose a cookie to make.

For each variation, after refrigeration, preheat the oven to 375°F, line your baking sheets with parchment paper, and bake for 12 to 15 minutes.

CHECKERBOARD

With your fingers, roll the dough into small (1/2-inch) rolls about 12-inches long. Place a cocoa roll next to a white roll. Put a cocoa on top of the white and a white on top of the cocoa. Wrap the whole thing in waxed paper and put it back into the refrigerator. Chill again for at least 1 hour. When you are ready to bake, trim the ends and slice 1/4-inch thick.

STRIPED

Divide the dough into halves again. (You should now have 4 sections total.) Put each of the 4 pieces between 2 sheets of parchment (approximately 12 x 14-inches)

and roll with a rolling pin into 3 1/2 x 12-inch rectangles. Transfer the flattened dough to baking sheets (without removing the parchment paper) and put it all back into the refrigerator. Chill again for at least 1 hour.

Take out the dough and remove the top pieces of parchment. One by one, place the layers on top of one another, alternating the cocoa and white layers, removing the parchment as you go. Cover with waxed paper and chill for another hour. When you are ready to bake, trim the ends and slice 1/4-inch thick.

CONCENTRIC CIRCLES

Divide the dough into halves again. (You should now have 4 sections total.) Take 1 of the white pieces and 1 of the cocoa pieces and put each of these between 2 sheets of parchment (approximately 12 x 14-inches). Roll with a rolling pin into 7 x 12-inch rectangles. Transfer the rectangles to baking sheets (without removing parchment paper) and put them into the refrigerator. Chill again for at least 1 hour.

Take the remaining sections of white and cocoa and divide each into 2 pieces, one twice the size of the other. (In addition to those in the refrigerator,

you will now have 2 pieces of cocoa and 2 of white.) Take the larger sections and put each of these pieces between 2 sheets of parchment (approximately 12 x 14-inches) and roll with a rolling pin into 4 1/2 x 12-inch rectangles. Transfer them to baking sheets (without removing parchment paper) and put them back into the refrigerator. Chill again for at least 1 hour. Take the last 2 small sections. Roll the cocoa into a 12-inch log. Wrap it in waxed paper. Do the same with the white. Put them back into the refrigerator. Chill again for at least 1 hour.

Remove the dough from the refrigerator and remove the top sheets of parchment from the rectangles. Place the white log (without the waxed paper!) in the middle of the smaller cocoa rectangle and wrap the cocoa rectangle around it. Repeat with the cocoa log and the white rectangle. Repeat this last step with the remaining two rectangles. Wrap both logs up in parchment or waxed paper and return them to the refrigerator. Chill again for at least 1 hour. When you are ready to bake, trim the ends and slice 1/4-inch thick.

About 3 dozen cookies

O Little Town of Bethlehem

1.

O Lit - tle Town of Beth - le - hem, How

still we __ see thee lie; A - bove thy deep and

dream - less sleep The si - lent __ stars go by; Yet

in thy dark streets shi - neth The ev - er - last - ing

light; The hopes and fears of all the years Are

met in thee to - - - night.

2. For Christ is born of Mary,
   And gathered all above,
   While mortals sleep, the angels keep
   Their watch of wond'ring love.
   O morning stars, together
   Proclaim the holy birth!
   And praises sing to God the King,
   And peace to men on earth!

3. How silently, how silently,
   The wondrous gift is giv'n!
   So God imparts to human hearts
   The blessing of his heav'n.
   No ear may hear His coming,

   But in this world of sin,
   Where meek souls will receive
     Him still,
   The dear Christ enters in.

4. O Holy child of Bethlehem!
   Descent to us, we pray;
   Cast out our sin, and enter in;
   Be born in us today.
   We hear the Christmas angels
   The great glad tidings tell;
   O come to us abide with us,
   Our Lord Emmanuel.

Once on Christmas

Dorothy Thompson

It is Christmas Eve—the festival that belongs to mothers and fathers and children, all over the so-called Western world. It's not a time to talk about situations, or conditions, or reactions, or people who emerge briefly into the news. My seven-year-old son asked me this evening to tell him what Christmas was like when I was a little girl, before people came home for Christmas in airplanes, thirty odd years ago. And so I told him this:

A long, long time ago, when your mother was your age, and not nearly as tall as you, she lived with her mother, and father, and younger brother, and little sister, in a Methodist parsonage, in Hamburg, New York. It was a tall wooden house, with a narrow verandah on the side, edged with curley-cues of woodwork at the top, and it looked across a lawn at the church where Father preached every Sunday morning and evening. In the backyard there were old Baldwin and Greening apple trees, and a wonderful, wonderful barn. But that is another story. The village now has turned into a suburb of the neighboring city of Buffalo, and fathers who work there go in and out every day on the trains and buses, but then it was just a little country town, supported by the surrounding farms.

Father preached in his main church there on Sunday mornings but in the afternoons he had to drive out to the neighboring village of Armor where there was just a little box of a church in the middle of the farming country. For serving both parishes, he received his house and one thousand dollars a year. But he didn't always get the thousand dollars. Sometimes the crops were bad, and the farmers had no money, and when the farmers had no money the village people didn't have any either. Then the farmers would come to us with quarters of beef, or halves of pigs, or baskets of potatoes, and make what they called a donation. My mother hated the word, and sometimes would protest, but my father would

laugh, and say, "Let them pay in what they can! We are all in the same boat together."

For weeks before Christmas we were very, very busy. Mother was busy in the kitchen, cutting up citron and sorting out raisins and clarifying suet for the Christmas pudding—and shooting all of us out of the room, when we crept in to snatch a raisin, or a bit of kernel from the butter-nuts that my little

brother was set to cracking on the woodshed floor, with an old-fashioned flat-iron.

I would lock myself into my little bed-room, to bend over a handkerchief that I was hem-stitching for my mother. It is very hard to hemstitch when you are seven years old, and the thread would knot, and break, and then one would have to begin again, with a little rough place, where one had started over. I'm afraid the border of that handkerchief was just one succession of knots and starts.

The home-made presents were only a tiny part of the work! There was the Christmas tree! Mr. Heist, from my father's Armor parish, had brought it from his farm, a

magnificent hemlock, that touched the ceiling. We were transported with admiration, but what a tree to trim! For there was no money to buy miles of tinsel and boxes of colored glass balls.

But in the pantry was a huge stone jar of popcorn. When school was over, in the afternoons, we all gathered in the back parlor, which was the family sitting room. The front parlor was a cold place, where portraits of John Wesley and Frances Willard hung on the walls, and their eyes, I remember, would follow a naughty child accusingly around the room. The sofas in that room were of walnut, with roses and grapes carved on their backs, just where they'd stick into your back, if you fidgeted in them, and were covered with horse-hair which was slippery when it was new, and tickly when it was old. But that room was given over to visits from the local tycoons who sometimes contributed to the church funds, and couples who came to be married.

The back parlor was quite, quite different. It had an ingrain carpet on the floor, with patterns of maple leaves, and white muslin curtains at the windows, and an assortment of chairs contributed by the Parsonage Committee. A Morris chair, I remember, and some rockers, and a fascinating cabinet which was a desk and a bookcase, and a chest of drawers, and a mirror, all in one.

In this room there was a round iron stove, a very jolly stove, a cozy stove that winked at you with its red isin-glass eyes. On top of this stove was a round iron plate, it was flat, and a wonderful place to pop corn. There was a great copper kettle, used for making maple syrup, and we shook the popper on the top of the stove—first I shook until my arm was tired, and then Willard shook, until he was tired, and even the baby shook. The corn popped, and we poured it into the kettle and emptied the kettle, and poured it full again, until there was a whole barrel-full of popcorn, as white and fluffy as the snow that carpeted the lawn between the parsonage and the church.

Then we each got a darning

needle, a big one, and a ball of string. We strung the popcorn into long, long ropes, to hang upon the tree. But that was only half of it! There were stars to be cut out of kindergarten paper, red and green, and silver, and gold, and walnuts to be wrapped in gold paper, or painted with gold paint out of the paint-box that I had been given for my birthday. One got the paint into one's finger-nails, and it smelled like bananas. And red apples to be polished, because a shiny apple makes a brave show on a tree. And when it was all finished, it was Christmas Eve.

For Christmas Eve we all wore our best clothes. Baby in a little challis dress as blue as her eyes, and I had a new pinafore of Swiss lawn that my Aunt Margaret had sent me from England. We waited, breathless, in the front parlor while the candles were lit.

Then my mother sat at the upright piano in a rose-red cashmere dress and played, and my father sang, in his lovely, pure, gay, tenor voice:

> *"It came upon a midnight clear*
> *That glorious song of old,*
> *From angles bending near the earth*
> *To touch their harps of gold."*

And then we all marched in. It is true that we had decorated the tree ourselves, and knew intimately everything on it, but it shone in the dark room like an angel, and I could see the angels bending down, and it was so beautiful that one could hardly bear it. We all cried, "Merry Christmas!" and kissed each other.

There were bundles under the tree, most alluring bundles! But they didn't belong to Christmas Eve. They were for the morning. Before the morning came three little children would sit sleepily in the pews of their father's church and hear words drowsily, and shift impatiently, and want to go to sleep in order to wake up very, very early!

And wake up early we did! The windows were still gray, and, oh, how cold the room was! The church janitor had come over at dawn to stoke the hot air furnace in the parsonage, but at its best it only heated the rooms directly above it, and the upstairs depended on grates in the floor, and the theory that heat rises. We shuddered out of our

beds, trembling with cold and excitement, and into our clothes, which, when I was a little girl, were very complicated affairs indeed. First, a long fleece-lined union suit, and then a ferris waist dripping with buttons, then the cambric drawers edged with embroidery, and a flannel petticoat handsome with scallops, and  another petticoat of cambric and embroidery, just for show, and over that a gay plaid dress, and a dainty pinafore. What polishing of cheeks, and what brushing of hair and then a grand tumble down the stairs into the warm, cozy back parlor.

Presents! There was my beloved Miss Jam-up with a brand new

195

head! Miss Jam-up was once a sweet little doll, dears, who had become badly battered about the face in the course of too affectionate ministrations, and here she was again, with a new head altogether and new clothes, and eyes that open and shut. Scarfs and mittens from my mother's lively fingers. A doll house made from a wooden cracker box and odds and ends of wall paper, with furniture cut from stiff cardboard—and that was mother's work, too. And a new woolen dress, and new pinafores!

Under the tree was a book: *The Water Babies*, by Charles Kingsley. *To my beloved daughter Dorothy.*

Books meant sheer magic. There were no automobiles—none for Methodist ministers, in those days. No moving pictures. No radio. But inside the covers of books was everything, everything, that exists outside in the world today. Lovely, lovely words of poetry, that slipped like colored beads along a string; tales of rose-red cities, half as old as time. All that men can imagine, and construct, and make others imagine.

One couldn't read the book now. But there it lay, the promise of a perfect afternoon. Before one could get at it, one would go into the dining room. And what a dinner! This Christmas there was Turkey— with best wishes from one of my father's parishioners. And the pudding, steaming, and with two kinds of sauce. And no one to say, "No, dear, I think one helping is enough."

We glutted ourselves, we distended ourselves, we ate ourselves into a coma, so that we all had to lie down and have a nap.

Then, lying before the stove, propped on my elbows, I opened the covers of my Christmas book.

"Once upon a time there was a little chimney sweep, and his name was Tom. He lived in a great town of the North Country . . . in England."

How well I knew that North Country, with its rows on rows of dark stone houses, its mine pits, its poor workmen. From such a town my father had come, across the ocean, to this village in upstate New York. I forgot Christmas, forgot everything, except the fate of little Tom. What a book! It wasn't just a story. There was poetry in it. The words of the poems sang in my head, so that after all these years

I can remember them:

When all the world is young, lad,
And all the trees are green;
And every goose, a swan, lad,
And every lass a Queen;
Then hey for boot and spur, lad,
And round the world away;
Young blood must have its course, lad,
And every dog his day.

The little girl lay and dreamed that all the world was wide and beautiful, filled only with hearts as warm and hands as tender, and spirits as generous as the only ones she had ever known . . . when she was seven years old.

I WISH YOU ALL A MERRY CHRISTMAS!
I WISH US ALL A WORLD AS KIND AS A
CHILD CAN IMAGINE IT!

❄

Hot Chocolate with Peppermint Sticks

*Y*ou can either use your favorite instant hot chocolate mix or try this recipe from scratch.

HOT CHOCOLATE:

whole milk (skim milk or water can be substituted)

your favorite unsweetened cocoa

white sugar

mini-marshmallows

peppermint sticks

1. Following portion directions on the packaging, combine milk and cocoa in a medium-size saucepan on low heat.

2. Using a handheld manual egg beater or whisk, whip the mixture as it heats until smoothly blended.

3. Hot Chocolate should now be warm but not boiling. Add sugar and continue to blend until hot.

Serve with tiny marshmallows or whipped cream and a peppermint candy cane. Nibble the candy cane between stirring.

WHIPPED CREAM:

1/2 pint whipping cream

1 teaspoon vanilla extract

1 teaspoon white sugar

1. Combine ingredients
in a mixing bowl.

2. Whip with an electric mixer
or by hand until stiff peaks form.

3. Spoon over steaming
Hot Chocolate.

Christmas at Hyde Park

Eleanor Roosevelt

When our children were young, we spent nearly every Christmas holiday at Hyde Park. We always had a party the afternoon of Christmas Eve for all the families who lived on the place. The presents were piled under the tree, and after everyone had been greeted, my husband would choose the children old enough to distribute gifts and send them around to the guests. My mother-in-law herself always gave out her envelopes with money, and I would give out ours. The cornucopias filled with old-fashioned sugar candies and the peppermint canes hanging on the trees were distributed, too, and then our guests would leave us and enjoy their ice cream, cake, and coffee or milk in another room. Later in the day, when the guests had departed, my husband would begin the reading of *A Christmas Carol*. He never read it through; but he would select parts he thought suitable for the youngest members of the family. Then, after supper, he would read other parts for the older ones.

On Christmas morning, I would get up and close the windows in our room, where all the stockings had been hung on the mantel. The little children would be put into our bed and given their stockings to open. The others would sit around the fire. I tried to see that they all had a glass of orange juice before the opening of stockings really began, but the excitement was so great I was not always successful.

Breakfast was late Christmas morning, and my husband resented having to go to church on Christmas Day and sometimes flatly refused to attend. But I would go with my mother-in-law and such children as she could persuade to accompany us. For the most part, however, the children stayed home. In later years, I went to midnight service on Christmas Eve, and we gave up going to church in the morning.

I remembered the excitement as each child grew old enough to have his own sled and would start out after breakfast to try it on the hill behind the stable. Franklin would go coasting with them, and until the children were nearly grown, he was the only one who ever piloted the bobsled down the hill. Everyone came in for a late lunch, and at dusk we would light the candles on the tree again. Only outdoor presents like sleds and skates were distributed in the morning. The rest were kept for the late-afternoon Christmas tree. Again they were piled under the tree, and my husband and the children scrambled around it, and he

203

called the names.

At first, my mother-in-law did a great deal of shopping and wrapping, and the Hyde Park Christmas always included her gifts. Later, she found shopping too difficult. Then she would give each person a check, though she managed very often to give her son the two things she knew he would not buy for himself—silk shirts and silk pajamas. These she bought in London, as a rule, and saved for his Christmas, which to her was always very special.

In the early years of our marriage, I did a great deal more sewing and embroidering than I've done since, so many of my gifts were things I had made. The family still has a few pieces of Italian cutwork embroidery and other kinds of my perfectly useless handwork. I look back, however,

with some pleasure on the early Hyde Park days, when I would have a table filled with pieces of silk and make sachets of different scents. I would dry pine needles at Campobello Island and make them into sweet-smelling bags for Christmas. Now I rarely give a present I have made, and perhaps, it is just as well, for what one buys is likely to be better made!

Each of the children had a special preference in gifts. When Anna was a small child, her favorite present was a rocking horse, on which she spent many hours. Later, she was to spend even more hours training her own horse, which her great-uncle Mr. Warren Delano gave her. One of the nicest gifts we could possibly give her as she grew older was something for her horse, Natomah. Jimmy loved boats from the very beginning,

whether he floated them in the bathtub or later competed with his father in the regattas of toy boats on the Hudson River. Elliott was always trying to catch up with his older brother and sister; but because he was delicate as a child, I think he read more than the others. I remember that books and games were very acceptable gifts for him. Franklin, Jr., and John were a pair and had to have pretty much the same things, or they would quarrel

over them. They had learned together to ride and to swim, so gifts for outdoor sports were always favorites of theirs.

My children teased me because their stockings inevitably contained toothbrushes, toothpaste, nail cleaners, soap, washcloths, etc. They said Mother never ceased to remind them that cleanliness was next to godliness—even on Christmas morning. In the toe of each stocking, I always put a purse, with a dollar bill for the young ones and a five-dollar bill for the older ones. These bills were hoarded to supplement the rather meager allowances they had. When I was able to buy sucre d'orge (barley sugar), I put that in their stockings, together with some old-fashioned peppermint sticks; but as they grew older, this confection seemed to vanish from the market, and I had

to give it up and substitute chocolates. The stockings also contained families of little china pigs or rabbits or horses, which the children placed on their bookshelves.

The children themselves could probably tell much better than I can the things they remember most about these years. But I know that all of them have carried on many of the Hyde Park Christmas traditions with their children. Today, some of my grandchildren are establishing the same customs, and my great-grandchildren will one day remember the same kind of Christmas we started so many years ago.

❄

Carol of the Field Mice

Kenneth Grahame

Villagers all, this frosty tide,
Let your doors swing open wide,
Though wind may follow, and snow beside,
Yet draw us in by your fire to bide;
   Joy shall be yours in the morning!

Here we stand in the cold and the sleet,
Blowing fingers and stamping feet,
Come from far away you to greet—
you by the fire and we in the street—
   Bidding you joy in the morning!

For ere one half of the night was gone,
Sudden a star has led us on,
Raining bliss and benison—
Bliss tomorrow and more anon,
    Joy for every morning!

Goodman Joseph toiled through the snow—
Saw the star o'er a stable low;
Mary she might not further go—
Welcome thatch, and litter below!
    Joy was hers in the morning!

And then they heard the angels tell
"Who were the first to cry Nowell?
Animals all, as it befell,
In the stable where they did dwell!
    Joy shall be theirs in the morning!"

A Miserable, Merry Christmas

Lincoln Steffens

My father's business seems to have been one of slow but steady growth. He and his local partner, Llewelen Tozer, had no vices. They were devoted to their families and to "the store," which grew with the town, from a gambling, mining, and ranching community to one of farming, fruit-raising, and building. Immigration poured in, not gold-seekers now, but farmers, businessmen and home-builders, who settled, planted, reaped, and traded in the natural riches of the State, which prospered greatly, "making" the people who will tell you that they "made the State."

As the store made money and I was getting through the primary school, my father bought a lot uptown, at Sixteenth and K Streets, and built us a "big" house. It was off the line of the city's growth, but it was near a new grammar school for me and my sisters, who were coming along fast after me. This interested the family, not me. They were always talking about school; they had not had much of it themselves, and they thought they had missed something. My father used to write speeches, my mother verses, and their theory seems to have been that they had talents which a school would have brought to flower. They agreed, therefore, that their children's gifts should have all the schooling there was. My view, then, was that I had had a good deal of it already, and I was not interested at all. It interfered with my own business, with my own education.

And indeed I remember very little of the primary school. I learned to read, write, spell, and count, and reading was all right. I had a practical use for books, which I searched for ideas and parts to play with, characters to be, lives to live. The primary school was probably a good one, but I cannot remember learning anything except to

read aloud "perfectly" from a teacher whom I adored and who was fond of me. She used to embrace me before the whole class and she favored me openly to the scandal of the other pupils, who called me "teacher's pet." Their scorn did not trouble me; I saw and I said that they envied me. I paid for her favor, however. When she married I had queer, unhappy feelings of resentment; I didn't want to meet her husband, and when I had to I wouldn't speak to him. He laughed, and she kissed me— happily for her, to me offensively. I never would see her again. Through with her, I fell in love immediately with Miss Kay, another grown young woman who wore glasses and had a fine, clear skin. I did not know her, I only saw her in the street, but once I followed her, found out where she lived, and used

to pass her house, hoping to see her, and yet choking with embarrassment if I did. This fascination lasted for years; it was still a sort of super-romance to me when later I was "going with" another girl nearer my own age.

What interested me in our new neighborhood was not the school, nor the room I was to have in the house all to myself, but the stable which was built back of the house. My father let me direct the making of a stall, a little smaller than the other stalls, for my pony, and I prayed and hoped and my sister Lou believed that that meant that I would get the pony, perhaps for Christmas. I pointed out to her that there were three other stalls and no horses at all. This I said in order that she should answer it. She could not. My father, sounded, said that some day we might have

horses and a cow; meanwhile a stable added to the value of a house. "Some day" is a pain to a boy who lives in and knows only "now." My good little sisters, to comfort me, remarked that Christmas was coming, but Christmas was always coming and grown-ups were always talking about it, asking you what you wanted and then giving you what they wanted you to have. Though everybody knew what I wanted, I told them all again. My mother knew that I told God, too, every night. I wanted a pony, and to make sure that they understood, I declared that I wanted nothing else.

"Nothing but a pony?" my father asked.

"Nothing," I said.

"Not even a pair of high boots?"

That was hard. I did want boots, but I stuck to the pony.

"No, not even boots."

"Nor candy? There ought to be something to fill your stocking with, and Santa Claus can't put a pony into a stocking."

That was true, and he couldn't lead a pony down the chimney either. But no. "All I want is a pony," I said. "If I can't have a pony, give me nothing, nothing."

Now I had been looking myself for the pony I wanted,

going to sales stables, inquiring of horsemen, and I had seen several that would do. My father let me "try" them. I tried so many ponies that I was learning fast to sit a horse. I chose several, but my father always found some fault with them. I was in despair. When Christmas was at

hand I had given up all hope of a pony, and on Christmas Eve I hung up my stocking along with my sisters', of whom, by the way, I now had three. I haven't mentioned them or their coming because, you understand, they were girls, and girls, young girls, counted for nothing in my manly life. They did not mind me either; they were so happy that Christmas Eve that I caught some of their merriment. I speculated on what I'd get; I hung up the biggest stocking I had, and we all went reluctantly to bed to wait till morning. Not to sleep; not right away. We were told that we must not only sleep promptly, we must not wake up till seven-thirty the next morning—or if we did, we must not go to the fireplace for our Christmas. Impossible.

We did sleep that night, but we woke up at six A.M. We lay in our

beds and debated through the open doors whether to obey till, say, half-past six. Then we bolted. I don't know who started it, but there was a rush. We all disobeyed; we raced to disobey and get first to the fireplace in the front room downstairs. And there they were, the gifts, all sorts of wonderful things, mixed-up piles of presents; only, as I disentangled the mess, I saw that my stocking was empty; it hung limp; not a thing in it; and under and around it—nothing. My sisters had knelt down, each by her pile of gifts; they were squealing with delight, till they looked up and saw me standing there in my nightgown with nothing. They left their piles to come to me and look with me at my empty place. Nothing. They felt my stocking: nothing.

I don't remember whether I cried at that moment, but my sisters did. They ran with me back to my bed, and there we all cried till I became indignant. That helped some. I got up, dressed, and driving my sisters away, I went alone out into the yard, down to the stable, and there, all by myself, I wept. My mother came out to me by and by; she found me in my pony stall, sobbing on the floor, and she tried to comfort me. But I heard my father outside; he had come part way with her, and she was having some sort of angry quarrel with him. She tried to comfort me; besought me to come to breakfast. I could not; I wanted no comfort and no breakfast. She left me and went on into the house with sharp words for my father.

I don't know what kind of a breakfast the family had. My sisters said it was "awful." They were ashamed to enjoy their own toys. They came to me, and I was rude. I ran away from them. I went around to the front of the house, sat down on the steps, and, the crying over, I ached. I was wronged, I was hurt—I can feel now what I felt then, and I am sure that if one could see the wounds upon our hearts, there would be found still upon mine a scar from that terrible Christmas morning. And my father, the practical joker, he must have been hurt, too, a little. I saw him looking out of the window. He was watching me or something for an hour or two, drawing back the curtain ever so little lest I catch him, but I saw his face, and I think I can see now the anxiety upon it, the worried impatience.

After—I don't know how long— surely an hour or two—I was brought to the climax of my agony by the sight of a man riding a pony down the street, a pony and a brand-new saddle; the most beautiful saddle I ever saw, and it was a boy's saddle; the man's feet were not in the stirrups; his legs were too long. The outfit was perfect; it was the realization of all my dreams, the answer to all my prayers. A fine new bridle, with a light curb bit. And the pony! As he drew near, I saw that the pony was really a small horse, what we called an Indian pony, a bay, with black mane and tail, and one white foot and a white star on his forehead. For such a horse as that I would have given, I could have forgiven, anything.

But the man, a disheveled fellow with a blackened eye and a fresh-cut face, came along, reading the numbers on the houses, and, as my hopes—my impossible hopes—rose, he looked at our door and passed by, he and the pony, and the saddle and the bridle. Too much. I fell upon the steps, and having wept before, I broke now into such a flood of tears that I was a floating wreck when I heard a voice.

"Say, kid," it said, "do you know a boy named Lennie Steffens?"

I looked up. It was the man on the pony, back again, at our horse block.

"Yes," I spluttered through my tears. "That's me."

"Well," he said, "then this is your horse. I've been looking all over for you and your house. Why don't you put your number where it can be seen?"

"Get down," I said, running out to him.

He went on saying something about "ought to have got here at seven o'clock; told me to bring the nag here and tie him to your post and leave him for you. But, hell, I got into a drunk—and a fight—and a hospital, and—"

"Get down," I said.

He got down, and he boosted me up to the saddle. He offered to fit the stirrups to me, but I didn't want him to. I wanted to ride.

"What's the matter with you?" he said, angrily. "What you crying for? Don't you like the horse? He's a dandy, this horse. I know him of old. He's fine at cattle; he'll drive 'em alone."

I hardly heard, I could scarcely wait, but he persisted. He adjusted the stirrups, and then, finally, off I rode, slowly, at a walk, so happy, so thrilled, that I did not know what I was doing. I did not look back at the house or the man, I rode off up the street, taking note of everything—of the reins, of the pony's long mane, of the carved leather saddle. I had never seen anything so beautiful. And mine! I was going to ride up past Miss Kay's house. But I noticed on the horn of the saddle some stains like rain-drops, so I turned and trotted home, not to the house but to the stable. There was the family, father, mother, sisters, all working for me, all happy. They had been putting in place the tools of my new business: blankets, currycomb, brush, pitchfork—everything, and there was hay in the loft.

"What did you come back so soon for?" somebody asked. "Why didn't you go on riding?"

I pointed to the stains. "I wasn't going to get my new saddle rained

on," I said. And my father laughed. "It isn't raining," he said. "Those are not rain-drops."

"They are tears," my mother gasped, and she gave my father a look which sent him off to the house. Worse still, my mother offered to wipe away the tears still running out of my eyes. I gave her such a look as she had given him, and she went off after my father, drying her own tears. My sisters remained and we all unsaddled the pony, put on his halter, led him to his stall, tied and fed him. It began really to rain; so all the rest of that memorable day we curried and

combed that pony. The girls plaited his mane, forelock, and tail, while I pitchforked hay to him and curried and brushed, curried and brushed. For a change we brought him out to drink; we led him up and down, blanketed like a race-horse; we took turns at that. But the best, the most inexhaustible fun, was to clean him. When we went reluctantly to our midday Christmas dinner, we all smelt of horse, and my sisters had to wash their faces and hands. I was asked to, but I wouldn't, till my mother bade me look in the mirror. Then I washed up—quick. My face was caked with the muddy lines of tears that had coursed over my cheeks to my mouth. Having washed away that shame, I ate my dinner, and as I ate I grew hungrier and hungrier. It was my first meal that day, and as I filled up on the turkey and the stuffing, the cranberries and the pies, the fruit and the nuts—as I swelled, I could laugh. My mother said I still choked and sobbed now and then, but I laughed, too; I saw and enjoyed my sisters' presents till—I had to go out and attend to my pony, who was there, really and truly there, the promise, the beginning, of a happy double life. And—I went and looked to make sure—there was the saddle, too, and the bridle.

But that Christmas, which my father had planned so carefully, was it the best or the worst I ever knew? He often asked me that; I never could answer as a boy. I think now that it was both. It covered the whole distance from broken-hearted misery to bursting happiness—too fast. A grown-up could hardly have stood it.

❄

The Twelve Days of Christmas

1.

On the first day of Christ-mas my true love gave to me, a par-tridge — in a pear tree. On the sec-ond day of Christ-mas my true love gave to me, Two tur-tle doves and a par-tridge— in a pear tree. On the

third day of Christ-mas my true love gave to me, Three French — hens,
fourth day of Christ-mas my true love gave to me, Four mock-ingbirds,

Two tur-tle doves and a par-tridge __ in a pear tree. On the

Three French __ hens, Two tur-tle doves and a par-tridge __ in a pear tree.

On the fifth day of Christ-mas my true love gave to me,

Five gold-en rings, Four __ mock-ing birds, Three French hens,

Two __ tur-tle doves, and a par-tridge __ in a pear tree.

On the sixth day of Christ-mas my true love gave to me,

Six geese a-lay-ing, Sev-en swans a-swim-ming, Six geese a-lay-ing,

Eight — maids a-milk-ing, Sev-en swans a-swim-ming, Six geese a-lay-ing,

9. The ninth day of Christmas my true love sent to me
   Nine ladies dancing,

10. The tenth day of Christmas my true love sent to me
    Ten lords a-leaping,

11. The eleventh day of Christmas my true love sent to me
    Eleven pipers piping,

12. The twelfth day of Christmas my true love sent to me
    Twelve drummers drumming,

Christmas Every Day

William Dean Howells

The little girl came into her papa's study, as she always did Saturday morning before breakfast, and asked for a story. He tried to beg off that morning, for he was very busy, but she would not let him. So he began:

"Well, once there was a little pig—"

She put her hand over his mouth and stopped him at the word. She said she had heard little pig stories till she was perfectly sick of them.

"Well, what kind of story *shall* I tell, then?"

"About Christmas. It's getting to be the season. It's past Thanksgiving already."

"It seems to me," argued her papa, "that I've told as often about Christmas as I have about little pigs."

"No difference! Christmas is more interesting."

"Well!" Her papa roused himself from his writing by a great effort. "Well, then, I'll tell you about the little girl that wanted it Christmas every day in the year. How would you like that?"

"First-rate!" said the little girl; and she nestled into comfortable shape in his lap, ready for listening.

"Very well, then, this little pig—Oh, what are you pounding me for?"

"Because you said little pig instead of little girl."

"I should like to know what's the difference between a little pig and a little girl that wanted it Christmas every day!"

"Papa," said the little girl, warningly, "if you don't go on, I'll *give* it to you!" And at this her papa darted off like lightning, and began to tell the story as fast as he could.

Well, once there was a little girl who liked Christmas so much that she wanted it to be Christmas every day in the year; and as soon as Thanksgiving was over she began

to send postal cards to the old Christmas Fairy to ask if she mightn't have it. But the old Fairy never answered any of the postals; and, after a while, the little girl found out that the Fairy was pretty particular, and wouldn't even notice anything but letters, not even correspondence cards in envelopes; but real letters on sheets of paper, and sealed outside with a monogram—or your initial, any way. So, then, she began to send her letters; and in about three weeks— or just the day before Christmas, it was—she got a letter from the Fairy, saying she might have it Christmas every day for a year, and then they would see about having it longer.

The little girl was a good deal excited already, preparing for the old-fashioned, once-a-year Christmas that was coming the next day, and perhaps the Fairy's promise didn't make such an impression on her as it would have made at some other time. She just resolved to keep it to herself, and surprise everybody with it as it kept coming true; and then it slipped out of her mind altogether.

She had a splendid Christmas. She went to bed early, so as to let Santa Claus have a chance at the stockings, and in the morning she was up the first of anybody and went and felt them, and found hers all lumpy with packages of candy, and oranges and grapes, and pocket-books and rubber balls and all kinds of small presents, and her big brother's with nothing but the tongs in them, and her young lady sister's with a new silk umbrella, and her papa's and mamma's with potatoes and pieces of coal wrapped up in tissue paper, just as they always had every Christmas. Then she waited around till the rest of the family were up, and she was the first to burst into the library, when the doors were opened, and look at the large presents laid out on the library-table—books, and portfolios, and boxes of stationery, and breast-pins, and dolls, and little stoves, and dozens of handkerchiefs, and ink-stands, and skates, and snow-shovels, and photograph-frames, and little easels, and boxes of watercolors, and Turkish paste, and

nougat, and candied cherries, and dolls' houses, and waterproofs—and the big Christmas-tree, lighted and standing in a waste-basket in the middle.

She had a splendid Christmas all day. She ate so much candy that she did not want any breakfast; and the whole forenoon the presents kept pouring in that the express-man had not had time to deliver the night before; and she went 'round giving the presents she had got for other people, and came home and ate turkey and cranberry for dinner, and plum-pudding and nuts and raisins and oranges and more candy, and then went out and coasted and came in with a stomach-ache, crying; and her papa said he would see if his house was turned into that sort of fool's paradise another year; and they had a light supper, and pretty early everybody went to bed cross.

Here the little girl pounded her papa in the back, again.

"Well, what now? Did I say pigs?"

"You made them *act* like pigs."

"Well, didn't they?"

"No matter; you oughtn't to put it into a story."

"Very well, then, I'll take it all out."

Her father want on:

The little girl slept very heavily, and she slept very late, but she was wakened at last by the other children dancing 'round her bed with their stockings full of presents in their hands.

"What is it?" said the little girl, and she rubbed her eyes and tried to rise up in bed.

"Christmas! Christmas! Christmas!" they all shouted,

229

and waved their stockings.

"Nonsense! It was Christmas yesterday."

Her brothers and sisters just laughed. "We don't know about that. It's Christmas to-day, any way. You come into the library and see."

Then all at once it flashed on the little girl that the Fairy was keeping her promise, and her year of Christmases was beginning. She was dreadfully sleepy, but she sprang up like a lark—a lark that had overeaten itself and gone to bed cross—and darted into the library. There it was again! Books, and portfolios, and boxes of stationery, and breast-pins—

"You needn't go over it all, Papa; I guess I can remember just what was there," said the little girl.

Well, and there was the Christmas-tree blazing away, and the family picking out their presents, but looking pretty sleepy, and her father perfectly puzzled, and her mother ready to cry. "I'm sure I don't see how I'm to dispose of all these things," said her mother, and her father said it seemed to him they had had something just like it the day before, but he supposed he must have dreamed it. This struck the little girl as the best kind of joke; and so she ate so much candy she didn't want any breakfast, and went 'round carrying presents, and had turkey and cranberry for dinner, and then went out and coasted, and came in with a—

"Papa!"
"Well, what now?"
"What did you promise,

you forgetful thing?"

"Oh! oh, yes!"

Well, the next day, it was just the same thing over again, but everybody getting crosser; and at the end of a week's time so many people had lost their tempers that you could pick up lost tempers everywhere; they perfectly strewed the ground. Even when people tried to recover their tempers they usually got somebody else's, and it

made the most dreadful mix.

The little girl began to get frightened, keeping the secret all to herself; she wanted to tell her mother, but she didn't dare to; and she was ashamed to ask the Fairy to take back her gift, it seemed ungrateful and ill-bred, and she thought she would try to stand it, but she hardly knew how she could, for a whole year. So it went on and on, and it was Christmas on St. Valentine's Day, and Washington's Birthday just the same as any day, and it didn't skip even the First of April, though everything was counterfeit that day, and that was some little relief.

After a while, coal and potatoes began to be awfully scarce, so many had been wrapped up in tissue paper to fool papas and mammas with. Turkeys got to be about a thousand dollars apiece—

"Papa!"

"Well, what?"

"You're beginning to fib."

"Well, *two* thousand, then."

And they got to passing off almost anything for turkeys—half-grown humming-birds, and even rocs out of the "Arabian Nights"—the real turkeys were so scarce. And cranberries—well, they asked a diamond apiece for cranberries. All the woods and orchards were cut down for Christmas-trees, and where the woods and orchards used to be, it looked just like a stubble-field, with the stumps. After a while they had to make Christmas-trees out of rags, and stuff them with bran, like old-fashioned dolls; but there were plenty of rags, because people got so poor, buying presents for one another, that they couldn't get any new clothes, and they just wore their old ones to tatters. They got so poor that everybody had to go to the poor-house, except the confectioners, and the fancy store-keepers, and the picture-booksellers, and the expressmen; and *they* all got so rich and proud that they would hardly wait upon a person when he came to buy; it was perfectly shameful!

Well, after it had gone on about three or four months, the little girl, whenever she came into the room in the morning and saw those great ugly lumpy stockings dangling at the fire-place, and the disgusting presents around everywhere, used to just sit down and burst out crying. In six months she was perfectly exhausted; she couldn't even cry any more; she just lay on the lounge and rolled her eyes and panted. About the beginning of October

she took to sitting down on dolls, wherever she found them—French dolls, or any kind—she hated the sight of them so; and by Thanksgiving she was crazy, and just slammed her presents across the room.

By that time people didn't carry presents around nicely any more.

They flung them over the fence, or through the window, or anything; and, instead of running their tongues out and taking great pains to write "For dear Papa," or "Mamma," or "Brother," or "Sister," or "Susie," or "Sammie," or "Billie," or "Bobby," or "Jimmie," or "Jennie," or whoever it was, and troubling to get the spelling right, and then signing their names, and "'Xmas, 188—,'" they used to write in the gift-books, "Take it, you horrid old thing!" and then go and bang it against the front door. Nearly everybody had built barns to hold their presents; but pretty soon the barns over-flowed, and then they used to let them lie out in the rain, or anywhere. Sometimes the police used to come and tell them to shovel their presents off the side-walk, or they would arrest them. "I thought you said everybody had gone to the poor-house," interrupted the little girl.

"They did go, at first," said her papa; "but after a while the poor-houses got so full that they had to send the people back to their own houses. They tried to cry, when they got back, but they couldn't make the least sound."

"Why couldn't they?"

"Because they had lost their voices, saying 'Merry Christmas' so much. Did I tell you how it was on the Fourth of July?"

"No; how was it?" And the little girl nestled closer, in expectation of something uncommon.

Well, the night before, the boys stayed up to celebrate, as they always do, and fell asleep before twelve o'clock, as usual, expecting to be wakened by the bells and cannon. But it was nearly eight o'clock before the first boy in the United States woke up, and then he found out what the trouble was. As soon as he could get his clothes on, he ran out of the house and smashed a big cannon-torpedo down on the pavement; but it didn't make any more noise than a damp wad of paper, and, after he tried about twenty or thirty more, he began to pick them up and look at them. Every single torpedo was a big raisin! Then he just streaked it upstairs, and examined his firecrackers and toy-pistol and two-dollar collection of fireworks and found that they were nothing but sugar and candy painted up to look like fireworks! Before ten o'clock, every boy in the United States found out that his Fourth of July things had turned into Christmas things; and then they just sat down and cried—they were so mad. There are about twenty million boys in the United States, and so you can imagine what a noise they made. Some men got together before night, with a little powder that hadn't turned

into purple sugar yet, and they said they would fire off *one* cannon, any way. But the cannon burst into a thousand pieces, for it was nothing but rock-candy, and some of the men nearly got killed. The Fourth of July orations all turned into Christmas carols, and when anybody tried to read the Declaration, instead of saying, "When in the course of human events it becomes necessary," he was sure to sing, "God rest you, merry gentlemen." It was perfectly awful.

The little girl drew a deep sigh of satisfaction. "And how was it at Thanksgiving?" she asked. Her papa hesitated. "Well, I'm almost afraid to tell you. I'm afraid you'll think it's wicked." "Well, tell, any way," said the little girl.

Well, before it came Thanksgiving, it had leaked out who had caused all these Christmases. The little girl had suffered so much that she had talked about it in her sleep; and after that, hardly anybody would play with her. People just perfectly despised her, because if it had not been for her greediness, it wouldn't have happened; and now, when it came Thanksgiving, and she wanted them to go to church, and have a squash-pie and turkey, and show their gratitude, they said that all the turkeys had been eaten up for her old Christmas dinners, and if she would stop the Christmases, they would see about the gratitude. Wasn't it dreadful? And the very next day the little girl began to send letters to the Christmas Fairy, and then telegrams, to stop it. But it didn't do any good; and then she got to calling at the Fairy's house, but the girl that came to the door always said "Not at home," or "Engaged," or "At dinner," or something like that; and so it went on till it came to the old once-a-year Christmas Eve. The little girl fell asleep, and when she woke up in the morning—

"She found it was all nothing but a dream," suggested the little girl.

"No, indeed!" said her papa. "It was all every bit true!"

"Well, what *did* she find out then?"

"Why, that it wasn't Christmas at last, and wasn't ever going to

be, any more. Now it's time for breakfast."

The little girl held her papa fast around the neck.

"You shan't go if you're going to leave it *so!*"

"How do you want it left?"

"Christmas once a year."

"All right," said her papa; and he went on again.

Well, there was the greatest rejoicing all over the country, and it extended clear up into Canada. The people met together everywhere, and kissed and cried for joy. The city carts went around and gathered up all the candy and raisins and nuts, and dumped them into the river; and it made the fish perfectly sick; and the whole United States, as far out as Alaska, was one blaze of bonfires, where the children were burning up their giftbooks and presents of all kinds. They had the greatest time!

The little girl went to thank the old Fairy because she had stopped it being Christmas, and she said she hoped she would keep her promise, and see that Christmas never, never came again. Then the Fairy frowned, and asked her if she was sure she knew what she meant; and the little girl asked her, why not? and the old Fairy said that now she was behaving just as greedily as ever, and she'd better look out. This made the little girl think it all over carefully again, and she said she would be willing to have it Christmas about once in a thousand years; and then she said a hundred, and then she said ten, and at last she got down to one. Then the Fairy said that was the good old way that had pleased people ever since Christmas began, and she was

agreed. Then the little girl said, "What're your shoes made of?" And the Fairy said, "Leather." And the little girl said, "Bargain's done forever," and skipped off, and hippity-hopped the whole way home, she was so glad.

"How will that do?" asked the papa.

"First-rate!" said the little girl; but she hated to have the story stop, and was rather sober. However, her mamma put her head in at the door, and asked her papa:

"Are you never coming to breakfast? What have you been telling that child?"

"Oh, just a moral tale."

The little girl caught him around the neck again.

"*We* know! Don't you tell *what*, Papa! Don't you tell *what!*"

❄

Angels We Have Heard on High

1.

An - gels We Have Heard on High, Sweet - ly sing - ing o'er the plain,

And the moun - tains in re - ply, Ech - o - ing their joy - ous strain.

Refrain

Glo - - - - - - - - - - - - - - - ri - a in ex - cel - sis

De - o, Glo - - - - - - - - - - - - - - - ri - a

in ex - cel - sis De - - - - - o! _____

2. Shepherds, why this jubilee?
   Why your joyful strains prolong?
   What the gladsome tidings be
   Which inspire your heav'nly song?

   Refrain

3. Come to Bethlehem and see
   Him whose birth the angels sing;
   Come adore on bended knee
   Christ, the Lord, the new-born King.

Refrain

4. See Him in a manger laid,
   Whom the choir of angels praise;
   Holy Spirit, lend thine aid,
   While our hearts in love we raise.

Refrain

243

Traditional Pecan Pie

This is a holiday classic that we guarantee will be a crowd pleaser every time.

PASTRY:

1/4 pound plus 4 tablespoons
     unsalted butter

3 cups all-purpose flour

3 tablespoons sugar

2 egg yolks, lightly beaten

About 1/4 cup ice water

FILLING:

5 whole eggs

1 egg yolk

1 cup packed light brown sugar

2 tablespoons melted butter

2 teaspoons vanilla extract

2 to 3 tablespoons bourbon

3 cups pecan pieces, lightly toasted

1. In a mixing bowl, cut butter into the flour until it reaches the consistency of fine meal.

2. Sprinkle on the sugar and add lightly beaten egg yolks and ice water. Lightly blend together. Firm the dough into a ball, wrap in waxed paper, and chill for at least 20 minutes.

3. Preheat oven to 350°F.

4. In a bowl, mix together all the filling ingredients except the pecans and blend well.

5. Roll out pastry on a lightly floured surface and fit it into a 9" pie pan. Evenly coat the pastry with the pecan pieces. Pour filling mixture over the nuts. Bake for 1 hour, or until golden brown.

6. Cool to room temperature before serving.

Serves 8 to 10

Napa Valley Apple Cranberry Crisp

*T*his recipe was inspired by the crisp made with oatmeal at
Mustards, a great restaurant in Napa Valley, California.
Nectarines or plums can be substituted for apples, with delicious results.

FILLING:

7 Granny Smith apples, cored
   and cut into slices
Juice from 2 lemons
2 cups fresh or frozen cranberries
$1/2$ cup white sugar

TOPPING:

1 cup oats
$1^1/2$ cups brown sugar
$1/2$ cup white flour
$1/2$ cup walnut nuggets
1 teaspoon cinnamon
$1/2$ teaspoon nutmeg
$1/2$ cup (1 stick) butter

1. Preheat the oven to 375°F.

2. Mix together the apples, lemon juice, cranberries, and white sugar. Put filling mixture into a 10 x 15-inch baking dish.

3. Mix the topping ingredients in a large bowl, cutting in the butter. Pour the topping mixture evenly over the filling.

4. Bake covered for 30 minutes, and uncovered for 30 minutes. Let cool for 15 minutes.

Serves 8 to 10

A Carol for Children

Ogden Nash

God rest you merry, Innocents,
Let nothing you dismay,
Let nothing wound an eager heart
Upon this Christmas day.

Yours be the genial holly wreaths,
The stockings and the tree;
An aged world to you bequeaths
Its own forgotten glee.

Soon, soon enough come crueler gifts,
The anger and the tears;
Between you now there sparsely drifts
A handful yet of years.

Oh, dimly, dimly glows the star
Through the electric throng;
The bidding in temple and bazaar
Drowns out the silver song.

The ancient altars smoke afresh,
The ancient idols stir;

Faint in the reek of burning flesh
Sink frankincense and myrrh.

Gaspar, Balthazar, Melchior!
Where are your offerings now?
What greetings to the Prince of War,
His darkly branded brow?

Two ultimate laws alone we know,
The ledger and the sword—
So far away, so long ago,
We lost the infant Lord.

Only the children clasp His hand;
His voice speaks low to them,
And still for them the shining band
Wings over Bethlehem.

God rest you merry, Innocents,
While Innocence endures.
A sweeter Christmas than we to ours
May you bequeath to yours.

A Christmas Dream, and How It Came True

Louisa May Alcott

I'm so tired of Christmas I wish there never would be another one!" exclaimed a discontented-looking little girl, as she sat idly watching her mother arrange a pile of gifts two days before they were to be given.

"Why, Effie, what a dreadful thing to say! You are as bad as old Scrooge; and I'm afraid something will happen to you, as it did to him, if you don't care for dear Christmas," answered mamma, almost dropping the silver horn she was filling with delicious candies.

"Who was Scrooge? What happened to him?" asked Effie, with a glimmer of interest in her listless face, as she picked out the sourest lemondrop she could find; for nothing sweet suited her just then.

"He was one of Dickens's best people, and you can read the charming story some day. He hated Christmas until a strange dream showed him how dear and beautiful it was, and made a better man of him."

"I shall read it; for I like dreams, and have a great many curious ones myself. But they don't keep me from being tired of Christmas," said Effie, poking discontentedly among the sweeties for something worth eating.

"Why are you tired of what should be the happiest time of all the year?" asked mamma, anxiously.

"Perhaps I shouldn't be if I had something new. But it is always the same, and there isn't any more surprise about it. I always find heaps of goodies in my stocking. Don't like some of them, and soon get tired of those I do like. We always have a great dinner, and I eat too much, and feel ill next day. Then there is a Christmas tree somewhere, with a doll on top, or a stupid old Santa Claus, and children dancing and screaming over bonbons and toys that break, and shiny things that are of no use. Really, mamma, I've had so many Christmases all alike that I don't think I *can* bear another one." And Effie laid herself flat on the sofa, as if the mere idea was too much for her.

Her mother laughed at her despair, but was sorry to see her little girl so discontented, when she had everything to make her happy, and had known but ten Christmas days.

"Suppose we don't give you *any* presents at all, —how would that suit you?" asked mamma, anxious to please her spoiled child.

"I should like one large and splendid one, and one dear little one, to remember some very nice person by," said Effie, who was a fanciful little body, full of odd whims and notions, which her friends loved to gratify, regardless of time, trouble, or money; for she was the last of three little girls, and very dear to all the family.

"Well, my darling, I will see what I can do to please you, and not say a word until all is ready. If I could only get a new idea to start with!" And mamma went on tying up her pretty bundles with a thoughtful face, while Effie strolled to the window to watch the rain that kept her indoors and made her dismal.

"Seems to me poor children have better times than rich ones. I can't go out, and there is a girl about my age splashing along, without any maid to fuss about rubbers and cloaks and umbrellas and colds. I wish I was a beggar-girl."

"Would you like to be hungry, cold, and ragged, to beg all day, and sleep on an ash-heap at night?" asked mamma, wondering what would come next.

"Cinderella did, and had a nice time in the end. This girl out here has a basket of scraps on her arm, and a big old shawl all round her, and doesn't seem to care a bit, though the water runs out of the toes of her boots. She goes paddling along, laughing at the rain, and eating a cold potato as if it tasted nicer than the chicken and ice-cream I had for dinner. Yes, I do think poor children are happier than rich ones."

"So do I, sometimes. At the Orphan Asylum to-day I saw two dozen merry little souls who have no parents, no home, and no hope of Christmas beyond a stick of candy or a cake. I wish you had been there to see how happy they were, playing with the old toys some richer children had sent them."

"You may give them all mine; I'm so tired of them I never want to see them again," said Effie, turning from the window to the pretty baby-house full of everything a child's heart could desire.

"I will, and let you begin again with something that you will not tire of, if I can only find it." And mamma knit her brows trying to discover some grand surprise for this child who didn't care for Christmas.

Nothing more was said then; and, wandering off to the library, Effie found "A Christmas Carol," and, curling herself up in the sofa corner, read it all before tea. Some of it she did not understand; but she laughed and cried over many parts of the charming story, and felt better without knowing why.

All the evening she thought of poor Tiny Tim, Mrs. Cratchit with the pudding, and the stout old gentleman who danced so gayly that "his legs twinkled in the air." Presently bedtime arrived.

"Come, now, and toast your feet," said Effie's nurse, "while I do your pretty hair and tell stories."

"I'll have a fairy tale to-night, a very interesting one," commanded Effie, as she put on her blue silk wrapper and little fur-lined slippers to sit before the fire and have her long curls brushed.

So Nursey told her best tales; and when at last the child lay down under her lace curtains, her head was full of a curious jumble of Christmas elves, poor children, snow-storms, sugar-plums and surprises. So it is no wonder that she dreamed all night, and this was the dream, which she never quite forgot.

She found herself sitting on a stone, in the middle of a great field, all alone. The snow was falling fast, a bitter wind whistled by, and night was coming on. She felt hungry, cold, and tired, and did not know where to go nor what to do.

"I wanted to be a beggar-girl, and now I am one; but I don't like it, and wish somebody would come and take care of me. I don't know who I am, and I think I must be lost," thought Effie, with the curious interest one takes in one's self in dreams.

But the more she thought about it, the more bewildered she felt. Faster fell the snow, colder blew the wind, darker grew the night; and poor Effie made up her mind that she was quite forgotten and left to freeze alone. The tears were chilled on her cheeks, her feet felt like icicles, and her heart died within her, so hungry, frightened, and forlorn was she. Laying her head on her knees, she gave herself up for lost, and sat there with the great flakes fast turning her to a little white mound, when suddenly the sound of music reached her, and starting up, she looked and listened with all her eyes and ears.

Far away a dim light shone, and a voice was heard singing. She tried to run toward the welcome

glimmer, but could not stir, and stood like a small statue of expectation while the light drew nearer, and the sweet words of the song grew clearer.

> *From our happy home*
> *Through the world we roam*
> *One week in all the year,*
> *Making winter spring*
> *With the joy we bring*
> *For Christmas-tide is here.*

> *Now the eastern star*
> *Shines from afar*
> *To light the poorest home;*
> *Hearts warmer grow,*
> *Gifts freely flow,*
> *For Christmas-tide has come.*

> *Now gay trees rise*
> *Before young eyes,*
> *Abloom with tempting cheer;*

> *Blithe voices sing,*
> *And blithe bells ring,*
> *For Christmas-tide is here.*

> *Oh, happy chime,*
> *Oh, blessed time,*
> *That draws us all so near!*
> *"Welcome, dear day,"*
> *All creatures say,*
> *For Christmas-tide is here.*

A child's voice sang, a child's hand carried the little candle and in the circle of soft light it shed, Effie saw a pretty child coming to her through the night and snow. A rosy, smiling creature, wrapped in white fur, with a wreath of green and scarlet holly on its shining hair, the magic candle in one hand and the

other outstretched as if to shower gifts and warmly press all other hands.

Effie forgot to speak as this bright vision came nearer, leaving no trace of footsteps in the snow, only lighting the way with its little candle, and filling the air with the music of its song.

"Dear child, you are lost, and I have come to find you," said the stranger, taking Effie's cold hands in his, with a smile like sunshine, while every holly berry glowed like a little fire.

"Do you know me?" asked Effie, feeling no fear, but a great gladness, at his coming.

"I know all children, and go to find them; for this is my holiday, and I gather them from all parts of the world to be merry with me once a year."

"Are you an angel?" asked Effie, looking for the wings.

"No; I am a Christmas spirit, and live with my mates in a pleasant place, getting ready for our holiday, when we are let out to roam about the world, helping make this a happy time for all who will let us in. Will you come and see how we work?"

"I will go anywhere with you. Don't leave me again," cried Effie, gladly.

"First I will make you comfortable. That is what we love to do. You are cold, and you shall be warm; hungry, and I will feed you; sorrowful, and I will make you gay."

With a wave of his candle all three miracles were wrought,—for the snow-flakes turned to a white fur cloak and hood on Effie's head and shoulders; a bowl of hot soup

came sailing to her lips, and vanished when she had eagerly drunk the last drop; and suddenly the dismal field changed to a new world so full of wonders that all her troubles were forgotten in a minute.

Bells were ringing so merrily that it was hard to keep from dancing. Green garlands hung on the walls, and every tree was a Christmas tree full of toys, and blazing with candles that never went out.

In one place many little spirits sewed like mad on warm clothes, turning off work faster than any sewing-machine ever invented, and great piles were made ready to be sent to poor people. Other busy creatures packed money into purses, and wrote checks which they sent flying away on the wind,—a lovely kind of snow-storm to fall into a world below full of poverty.

Older and graver spirits were looking over piles of little books, in which the records of the past year were kept, telling how different people had spent it, and what sort of gifts they deserved. Some got peace, some disappointment, some remorse and sorrow, some great joy and hope. The rich had generous thoughts sent them; the poor, gratitude and contentment. Children had more love and duty to parents; and parents renewed patience, wisdom, and satisfaction for and in their children. No one was forgotten.

"Please tell me what splendid place this is," asked Effie, as soon as she could collect her wits after the first look at all these astonishing things.

"This is the Christmas world; and here we work all the year round, never tired of getting ready for the happy day. See, these are the saints just setting off; for some have far to go, and the children must not be disappointed.

As he spoke the spirit pointed to four gates, out of which four great sleighs were just driving, laden with toys, while a jolly old Santa Claus sat in the middle of each, drawing on his mittens and tucking up his wraps for a long cold drive.

"Why, I thought there was only one Santa Claus, and even he was a humbug," cried Effie, astonished at the sight.

"Never give up your faith in the sweet old stories, even after you come to see that they are only the pleasant shadow of a lovely truth."

Just then the sleighs went off with a great jingling of bells and pattering of reindeer hoofs, while all the spirits gave a cheer that was heard in the lower world, where people said, "Hear the stars sing."

"I never will say there isn't any Santa Claus again. Now, show me more."

"You will like to see this place, I think, and may learn something here perhaps."

The spirit smiled as he led the way to a little door, through which Effie peeped into a world of dolls. Baby-houses were in full blast, with dolls of all sorts going on like live people. Waxen ladies sat in their parlors elegantly dressed; black dolls cooked in the kitchens; nurses walked out with the bits of dollies; and the streets were full of tin soldiers marching, wooden horses prancing, express wagons rumbling,

259

and little men hurrying to and fro. Shops were there, and tiny people buying legs of mutton, pounds of tea, mites of clothes, and everything dolls use or wear or want.

But presently she saw that in some ways the dolls improved upon the manners and customs of human beings, and she watched eagerly to learn why they did these things. A fine Paris doll driving in her carriage took up a black worsted Dinah who was hobbling along with a basket of clean clothes, and carried her to her journey's end, as if it were the proper thing to do. Another interesting china lady took off her comfortable red cloak and put it round a poor wooden creature done up in a paper shift, and so badly painted that its face would have sent some babies into fits.

"Seems to me I once knew a rich girl who didn't give her things to poor girls. I wish I could remember who she was, and tell her to be as kind as that china doll," said Effie, much touched at the sweet way the pretty creature wrapped up the poor fright, and then ran off in her little gray gown to buy a shiny fowl stuck on a wooden platter for her invalid mother's dinner.

"We recall these things to people's minds by dreams. I think the girl you speak of won't forget this one." And the spirit smiled, as if he enjoyed some joke which she did not see.

A little bell rang as she looked, and away scampered the children into the red-and-green school-house with the roof that lifted up, so one could see how nicely they sat at their desks with mites of books, or drew on the inch-square blackboards with crumbs of chalk.

"They know their lessons very well, and are as still as mice. We make a great racket at our school, and get bad marks every day. I shall tell the girls they had better mind what they do, or their dolls will be better scholars than they are," said Effie, much impressed, as she peeped in and saw no rod in the hand of the little mistress, who looked up and shook her head at the intruder, as if begging her to go away before the order of the school was disturbed.

Effie retired at once, but could not resist one look in at the window of a fine mansion, where the family were at dinner, the children behaved so well at table, and never grumbled a bit when their mamma said they could not have any more fruit.

"Now, show me something else," she said, as they came again to the low door that led out of Doll-land.

"You have seen how we prepare for Christmas; let me show you where we love best to send our good and happy gifts," answered the spirit, giving her his hand again.

"I know. I've seen ever so many," began Effie, thinking of her own Christmases.

"No, you have never seen what I will show you. Come away, and remember what you see to-night."

Like a flash that bright world vanished, and Effie found herself in a part of the city she had never seen before. It was far away from the gayer places, where every store was brilliant with lights and full of pretty things, and every house wore a festival air, while people hurried to and fro with merry greetings. It was down among the dingy streets where the poor lived, and where there was no making ready for Christmas.

Hungry women looked in at the shabby shops, longing to buy meat and bread, but empty pockets forbade. Tipsy men drank up their wages in the bar-rooms; and in many cold dark chambers little children huddled under the thin blankets, trying to forget their misery in sleep.

No nice dinners filled the air with savory smells, no gay trees dropped toys and bonbons into eager hands, no little stockings hung in rows beside the chimney-piece ready to be filled, no happy sounds of music, gay voices, and dancing feet were heard; and there were no signs of Christmas anywhere.

"Don't they have any in this place?" asked Effie, shivering, as she held fast the spirit's hand, following where he led her.

"We come to bring it. Let me show you our best workers." And the spirit pointed to some sweet-faced men and women who came stealing into the poor houses, working such beautiful miracles that Effie could only stand and watch.

Some slipped money into the empty pockets, and sent the happy mothers to buy all the comforts

they needed; others led the drunken men out of temptation, and took them home to find safer pleasures there. Fires were kindled on cold hearths, tables spread as if by magic, and warm clothes wrapped round shivering limbs. Flowers suddenly bloomed in the chambers of the sick; old people found themselves remembered; sad hearts were consoled by a tender word, and wicked ones softened by the story of Him who forgave all sin.

But the sweetest work was for the children; and Effie held her breath to watch these human fairies hang up and fill the little stockings without which a child's Christmas is not perfect, putting in things that once she would have thought very humble presents, but which now seemed beautiful and precious because these poor babies had nothing.

"That is so beautiful! I wish I could make merry Christmases as these good people do, and be loved and thanked as they are," said Effie, softly, as she watched the busy men and women do their work and steal away without thinking of any reward but their own satisfaction.

"You can if you will. I have shown you the way. Try it, and see how happy your own holiday will be hereafter."

As he spoke, the spirit seemed to put his arms about her, and vanished with a kiss.

"Oh, stay and show me more!" cried Effie, trying to hold him fast.

~

"Darling, wake up, and tell me why you are smiling in your sleep," said a voice in her ear; and, opening her eyes, there was mamma bending over her, and morning sunshine streaming into the room.

"Are they all gone? Did you hear the bells? Wasn't it splendid?" she asked, rubbing her eyes, and looking about her for the pretty child who was so real and sweet.

"You have been dreaming at a great rate,—talking in your sleep, laughing, and clapping you hands as if you were cheering some one. Tell me what was so splendid," said mamma, smoothing the tumbled hair and lifting up the sleepy head.

Then, while she was being dressed, Effie told her dream, and Nursey thought it very wonderful; but mamma smiled to see how curiously

things the child had thought, read, heard, and seen through the day were mixed up in her sleep.

"The spirit said I could work lovely miracles if I tried; but I don't know how to begin, for I have no magic candle to make feasts appear, and light up groves of Christmas trees, as he did," said Effie, sorrowfully.

"Yes, you have. We will do it! we will do it!" And clapping her hands, mamma suddenly began to dance all over the room as if she had lost her wits.

"How? how? You must tell me, mamma," cried Effie, dancing after her, and ready to believe anything possible when she remembered the adventures of the past night.

"I've got it! I've got it!—the new idea. A splendid one, if I can only carry it out!" And mamma waltzed the little girl round till her curls flew wildly in the air, while Nursey laughed as if she would die.

"Tell me! tell me!" shrieked Effie.

"No, no; it is a surprise,—a grand surprise for Christmas day!" sung mamma, evidently charmed with her happy thought. "Now, come to breakfast; for we must work like bees if we want to play spirits to-morrow. You and Nursey will go out shopping, and get heaps of things, while I arrange matters behind the scenes."

They were running downstairs as mamma spoke, and Effie called out breathlessly,—

"It won't be a surprise; for I know you are going to ask some poor children here, and have a tree or something. It won't be like my dream; for they had ever so many trees, and more children than

we can find anywhere."

"There will be no tree, no party, no dinner, in this house at all, and no presents for you. Won't that be a surprise?" And mamma laughed at Effie's bewildered face.

"Do it. I shall like it, I think; and I won't ask any questions, so it will all burst upon me when the time comes," she said; and she ate her breakfast thoughtfully, for this really would be a new sort of Christmas.

All that morning Effie trotted after Nursey in and out of shops, buying dozens of barking dogs, woolly lambs, and squeaking birds; tiny tea-sets, gay picture-books, mittens and hoods, dolls and candy. Parcel after parcel was sent home; but when Effie returned she saw no trace of them,

267

though she peeped everywhere. Nursey chuckled, but wouldn't give a hint, and went out again in the afternoon with a long list of more things to buy; while Effie wandered forlornly about the house, missing the usual merry stir that went before the Christmas dinner and the evening fun.

As for mamma, she was quite invisible all day, and came in at night so tired that she could only lie on the sofa to rest, smiling as if some very pleasant thought made her happy in spite of weariness.

"Is the surprise going on all right?" asked Effie, anxiously; for it seemed an immense time to wait till another evening came.

"Beautifully! better than I expected; for several of my good friends are helping, or I couldn't have done it as I wish. I know you will like it, dear, and long remember this new way of making Christmas merry."

Mamma gave her a very tender kiss, and Effie went to bed.

The next day was a very strange one; for when she woke there was no stocking to examine, no pile of gifts under her napkin, no one said "Merry Christmas!" to her, and the dinner was just as usual to her. Mamma vanished again, and Nursey kept wiping her eyes and saying: "The dear things! It's the prettiest idea I ever heard of. No one but your blessed ma could have done it."

"Do stop, Nursey, or I shall go crazy because I don't know the secret!" cried Effie, more than once; and she kept her eye on the clock, for at seven in the evening the surprise was to come off.

The longed-for hour arrived at

last, and the child was too excited to ask questions when Nurse put on her cloak and hood, led her to the carriage, and they drove away, leaving their house the one dark and silent one in the row.

"I feel like the girls in the fairy tales who are led off to strange places and see fine things," said Effie, in a whisper, as they jingled through the gay streets.

"Ah, my deary, it *is* like a fairy tale, I do assure you, and you *will* see finer things than most children will to-night. Steady, now, and do just as I tell you, and don't say one word, whatever you see," answered Nursey, quite quivering with excitement as she patted a large box in her lap, and nodded and laughed with twinkling eyes.

They drove into a dark yard, and Effie was led through a back door to a little room, where Nurse coolly proceeded to take off not only her cloak and hood, but her dress and shoes also. Effie stared and bit her lips, but kept still until out of the box came a little white fur coat and boots, a wreath of holly leaves and berries, and a candle with a frill of gold paper round it. A long "Oh!" escaped her then; and when she was dressed and saw herself in the glass, she started back, exclaiming, "Why, Nursey, I look like the spirit in my dream!"

"So you do; and that's the part you are to play, my pretty! Now whist, while I blind your eyes and put you in your place."

"Shall I be afraid?" whispered Effie, full of wonder; for as they went out she heard the sound of many voices, the tramp of many feet, and in spite of the bandage, was sure a great light shone upon her when she stopped.

"You needn't be; I shall stand close by, and your ma will be there."

After the handkerchief was tied about her eyes, Nurse led Effie up some steps, and placed her on a high platform, where something like leaves touched her head, and the soft snap of lamps seemed to fill the air.

Music began as soon as Nurse clapped her hands, the voices outside sounded nearer, and the tramp was evidently coming up the stairs.

"Now, my precious, look and see how you and your dear ma have made a merry Christmas for them

that needed it!"

Off went the bandage; and for a minute Effie really did think she was asleep again, for she actually stood in "a grove of Christmas trees," all gay and shining as in her vision. Twelve on a side, in two rows down the room, stood the little pines, each on its low table; and behind Effie a taller one rose to the roof, hung with wreaths of popcorn, apples, oranges, horns of candy, and cakes of all sorts, from sugary hearts to gingerbread Jumbos. On the smaller trees she saw many of her own discarded toys and those Nursey bought, as well as heaps that seemed to have rained down straight from that delightful Christmas country where she felt as if she were again.

"How splendid! Who is it for? What is that noise? Where is mamma?" cried Effie, pale with

271

pleasure and surprise, as she stood looking down the brilliant little street from her high place.

Before Nurse could answer, the doors at the lower end flew open, and in marched twenty-four little blue-gowned orphan girls, singing sweetly, until amazement changed the song to cries of joy and wonder as the shining spectacle appeared. While they stood staring with round eyes at the wilderness of pretty things about them, mamma stepped up beside Effie, and holding her hand fast to give her courage, told the story of the dream in a few simple words, ending in this way:—

"So my little girl wanted to be a Christmas spirit too, and make this a happy day for those who had not as many pleasures and comforts as she has. She like surprises, and we planned this for you all. She shall play the good fairy, and give each of you something from this tree, after which every one will find her own name on a small tree, and can go to enjoy it in her own way. March by, my dears, and let us fill your hands."

Nobody told them to do it, but all the hands were clapped heartily before a single child stirred; then one by one they came to look up wonderingly at the pretty giver of the feast as she leaned down to offer them great yellow oranges, red apples, bunches of grapes, bonbons, and cakes, till all were gone, and a double row of smiling faces turned toward her as the children filed back to their places in the orderly way they had been taught.

Then each was led to her own tree by the good ladies who had helped mamma with all their hearts; and the happy hubbub that arose would have satisfied even

273

Santa Claus himself,—shrieks of joy, dances of delight, laughter and tears (for some tender little things could not bear so much pleasure at once, and sobbed with mouths full of candy and hands full of toys). How they ran to show one another the new treasures! how they peeped and tasted, pulled and pinched, until the air was full of queer noises, the floor covered with papers, and the little trees left bare of all but candles!

"I don't think heaven can be any gooder than this," sighed one small girl, as she looked about her in blissful maze, holding her full apron with one hand, while she luxuriously carried sugarplums to her mouth with the other.

"Is that a truly angel up there?" asked another, fascinated by the little white figure with the wreath on its shining hair, who in some mysterious way had been the cause of all this merry making.

"I wish I dared to go and kiss her for this splendid party," said a lame child, leaning on her crutch, as she stood near the steps, wondering how it seemed to sit in a mother's lap, as Effie was doing, while she watched the happy scene before her.

Effie heard her, and remembering Tiny Tim, ran down and put her arms about the pale child, kissing the wistful face, as she said sweetly "You may; but mamma deserves the thanks. She did it all; I only dreamed about it."

Lame Katy felt as if "a truly angel" was embracing her, and could only stammer out her thanks, while the other children ran to see the pretty spirit, and touch her soft dress, until she stood in a crowd of blue gowns laughing as they held up their gifts for her to see and admire.

Mamma leaned down and whispered one word to the older girls; and suddenly they all took hands to dance round Effie, singing as they skipped.

It was a pretty sight, and the ladies found it hard to break up the happy revel; but it was late for small people, and too much fun is a mistake. So the girls fell into line, and marched before Effie and mamma again, to say goodnight with such grateful little faces that the eyes of those who looked grew dim with tears. Mamma kissed every one; and many a hungry childish heart felt as if the touch of those tender lips was their best gift. Effie shook so many small hands that her own tingled; and when Katy came she pressed a small doll into Effie's hand, whispering, "You didn't have a single present, and we had lots.

Do keep that; it's the prettiest thing I got."

"I will," answered Effie, and held it fast until the last smiling face was gone, the surprise all over, and she safe in her own bed, too tired and happy for anything but sleep.

"Mamma, it *was* a beautiful surprise, and I thank you so much! I don't see how you did it; but I like it best of all the Christmases I ever had, and mean to make one every year. I had my splendid big present, and here is the dear little one to keep for love of poor Katy; so even that part of my wish came true."

And Effie fell asleep with a happy smile on her lips, her one humble gift still in her hand, and a new love for Christmas in her heart that never changed through a long life spent in doing good.

❄

Deck the Halls

1.

Deck the Halls with boughs of hol-ly, Fa la la la la la la la la.

'Tis the sea-son to be jol-ly, Fa la la la la la la la la.

Don we now our gay ap-par-el, Fa la la la la la la la la.

Troll the an-cient Yule-tide car-ol, Fa la la la la la la la la.

278

2. See the blazing Yule before us, Fa la la la la la la la la.
Strike the harp and join the chorus, Fa la la la la la la la la.
Follow me in merry measure, Fa la la la la la la la la.
While I tell of Yuletide treasure, Fa la la la la la la la la.

3. Fast away the old year passes, Fa la la la la la la la la.
Hail the new, ye lads and lasses, Fa la la la la la la la la.
Sing we joyous all together, Fa la la la la la la la la.
Heedless of the wind and weather, Fa la la la la la la la la.

Snow Icing

*T*his icing is exquisite for decorating. It is a beautiful white, hardens perfectly, and tastes delicious. See icing tips on page 351.

1 package (16 oz) confectioners' sugar

3 egg whites

1 tablespoon white vinegar

Assorted food coloring

1. Place the confectioners' sugar in a mixing bowl.

2. In a separate bowl, beat the egg whites lightly with a fork. Add them to the sugar and beat with an electric mixer on the lowest speed for 1 minute. Add vinegar and beat for 2 more minutes at high speed, or until the mixture is stiff and glossy, as for stiff meringue.

3. Separate the mixture into small bowls and tint with different colors.

A Pint of Judgment

Elizabeth Morrow

The Tucker family made out lists of what they wanted for Christmas. They did not trust to Santa Claus' taste or the wisdom of aunts and uncles in such an important matter. By the first week in December everybody had written out what he or she hoped to receive.

Sally, who was seven, when she could only print had sent little slips of paper up the chimney with her desires plainly set forth. She had wondered sometimes if neatly written requests like Ellen's were not more effective than the printed ones. Ellen was eight. She had asked last year for a muff and Santa had sent it.

Mother always explained that one should not expect to get all the things on the list; "Only what you want most, dear, and sometimes you have to wait till you are older for those."

For several years Sally had asked for a lamb and she had almost given up hope of finding one tied to her stocking on Christmas morning. She had also asked for a white cat and a dove and they had not come either. Instead a bowl of goldfish had been received. Now she wrote so plainly that there was no excuse for misunderstandings like this.

Derek still printed his list—he was only six and yet he had received an Indian suit the very first time he asked for it. It was puzzling.

Caroline, called "Lovey" for short, just stood on the hearth rug and shouted "Dolly! Bow wow!" but anybody with Santa Claus' experience would know that rag dolls and woolly dogs were the proper presents for a four-year-old.

The lists were useful too in helping one to decide what to make for Father and Mother and the others for Christmas. The little Tuckers had been brought up by their grandmother in the belief that a present you made yourself was far superior to one bought in a store. Mother always asked for a great many things the children could make. She was always wanting knitted washcloths, pincushion covers, blotters and penwipers. Father needed pipe cleaners, calendars and decorated match boxes.

This year Sally longed to do something quite different for her mother. She was very envious of Ellen, who had started a small towel as her present, and was pulling threads for a fringed end.

"Oh! Ellen! How lovely that is!" she sighed. "It is a real grown-up present, just as if Aunt Elsie had made it."

"And it isn't half done yet," Ellen answered proudly. "Grandma is helping me with cross-stitch letters in blue and red for one end."

"If I could only make something nice like that! Can't you think of something for me?"

"A hemmed handkerchief?" suggested Ellen.

"Oh, no! Mother has lots of handkerchiefs."

"Yes, but when I gave her one for her birthday she said she had never had enough handkerchiefs. They were like asparagus."

"They don't look like asparagus," Sally replied, loath to criticize her mother but evidently confused. "Anyway, I don't want to give her a handkerchief."

"A penwiper?"

"No, I'm giving Father that."

"A new pincushion cover?"

"Oh! no, Ellen. I'm sick of those presents. I want it to be a big— lovely—Something—a great surprise."

Ellen thought a minute. She was usually resourceful and she did not like to fail her little sister. They had both been earning money all through November and perhaps this was a time to *buy* a present for Mother—even if Grandma disapproved.

"I know that Mother has made out a new list," she said. "She and Father were laughing about it last night in the library. Let's go and see if it is there."

They found two papers on the desk, unmistakably lists. They were typewritten. Father's was very short: "Anything wrapped up in tissue paper with a red ribbon around it."

"Isn't Father funny?" giggled Ellen. "I'd like to fool him and do up a dead mouse for his stocking."

Mother had filled a full page with her wants. Ellen read out slowly:

Pair of Old English silver peppers
Fur coat
("Father will give her that.")
Umbrella

Robert Frost's Poems
Silk stockings
Muffin tins
Small watering pot for house plants
Handkerchiefs
Guest towels
("Aren't you glad she asked for
that?" Sally broke in.)
Knitted wash cloths
A red pencil
A blue pencil
Ink eraser
Pen holders
Rubber bands
Hot water bag cover
A quart of judgment

This last item was
scribbled in
pencil at the
bottom
of the
sheet.

As Ellen finished reading, she
said with what Sally called her
"little-mother air," "You needn't
worry at all about Mother's present.
There are lots of things here you
could make for her. Couldn't you
do a hot water bag cover if
Grandma cut it out for you? I'm
sure you could. You take a nice soft
piece of old flannel. . . ."

"No! No! Nothing made out of
old flannel!" cried Sally. "That's
such a baby thing. I want it to be
different—and a great surprise. I
wish I could give her the silver
peppers. . . . That's the first thing on
her list; but I've only got two
dollars and three cents in my bank
and I'm afraid that's not enough."

"Oh! It isn't the peppers she
wants most!" cried Ellen. "It's the
last thing she wrote down—that
'quart of judgment.' I know for I
heard her tell Father, 'I need that

more than anything else . . . even a pint would help.' And then they both laughed."

"What is judgment?" asked Sally.

"It's what the judge gives—a judgment," her sister answered. "It must be something to do with the law."

"Then I know it would cost more than two dollars and three cents," said Sally. "Father said the other day that nothing was so expensive as the law."

"But she only asked for a pint," Ellen objected. "A pint of anything couldn't be very expensive, unless it was diamonds and rubies."

"She wanted a *quart*," Sally corrected. "And she just said that afterwards about a pint helping because she knew a whole quart would be too much for us to buy."

"A hot water bag cover would be lots easier," cautioned Ellen.

"I don't want it to be easy!" cried Sally. "I want it to be what she wants!"

"Well, perhaps you could get it cheap from Uncle John," Ellen suggested. "He's a lawyer—and he's coming to dinner tonight, so you could ask him."

Sally was not afraid to ask Uncle John anything. He never laughed at her or teased her as Uncle Tom sometimes did and he always talked to her as if she were grown up. On any vexed question he always sided with her and Ellen. He had even been known to say before Mother

that coconut cake was good for
children and that seven-thirty for
big girls of seven and eight was a
disgracefully early bedtime. He
thought arctics unnecessary in
winter and when a picnic was
planned, he always knew it would
be a fine day.

Sally drew him into the little
library that evening and shut the
door carefully.

"Is it something very important?"
he asked as they seated themselves
on the sofa.

"Yes," she answered. "Awfully
important. It's a secret. You won't
tell, will you?"

"No, cross my heart and swear.
What is it?"

"It's—it's . . . Oh—Uncle John—
what *is* judgment? I must get some."

"Judgment? That *is* an important
question, my dear." Uncle John
seemed puzzled for a moment.

"And it is hard to answer. Why do
you bother about that now? You
have your whole life to get it. . . .
Come to me again when you're
eighteen."

"But I can't wait so long. I must
get it right away. Mother wants if
for a Christmas present. She put on
her list, 'A quart of judgment.' She
said even a pint would help."

Uncle John laughed. He threw
back his head and shouted. Sally
had never seen him laugh so hard.
He shook the sofa with his mirth
and tears rolled down his cheeks.
He didn't stop until he saw that
Sally was hurt—and even then a
whirlwind of chuckles seized him
occasionally.

"I'm not laughing at you, Sally
darling," he explained at last,
patting her shoulder affectionately,
"but at your mother. She doesn't
need judgment. She has it. She

287

always has had it. She's a mighty fine woman—your mother. She must have put that on her list as a joke."

"Oh no! Excuse me, Uncle John," Sally protested. "She told Father she wanted it more than anything else. Wouldn't it be a good Christmas present?"

"Perfectly swell," her uncle answered. "The most useful. If you have any left over, give me some."

"Why, I was going to ask you to sell me some," Sally explained. "Ellen said you would surely have it."

Just then Mother called "Ellen! Sally! Bedtime. Hurry, dears. It's twenty minutes to eight already."

"Bother!" exclaimed Sally. "I'm always having to go to bed. But please tell me where I can get it. At Macy's? Delia is taking us to town tomorrow."

"No, my dear," he answered.

"Macy sells almost everything but not that. It doesn't come by the yard."

"Girls!" Mother's voice again.

"Oh! Quick, Uncle John," whispered Sally. "Mother's coming. I'll have to go. Just tell me. What *is* judgment?"

"It is *sense*, Sally," he answered, quite solemn and serious now. "Common sense. But it takes a lot. . . ." He could not finish the sentence for at this point Mother opened the door and carried Sally off to bed.

The little girl snuggled down under the sheets very happily. Uncle John had cleared her mind of all doubt. She had only time for an ecstatic whisper to Ellen before Delia put out the light: "It's all right about Mother's present. Uncle John said it would be 'swell.'" Then she began to calculate: "If it is just cents, common cents, I have ever so many in my bank and I can earn some more. Perhaps I have enough already."

With this delicious hope she fell asleep.

The first thing after breakfast the next morning she opened her bank. It was in the shape of a fat man sitting in a chair. When you put a penny in his hand he nodded his head in gratitude as the money slipped into his safetybox. Sally unscrewed the bottom of this and two dollars and three cents rolled out. It was not all in pennies. There

were several nickels, three dimes, two quarters and a fifty-cent piece. It made a rich-looking pile. Sally ran to the kitchen for a pint cup and then up to the nursery to pour her wealth into it. No one was there in the room to hear her cry of disappointment. The coins did not reach to the "Half" marked on the measure.

But there was still hope. The half dollar and quarters when they were changed would lift the level of course. She put all the silver into her pocket and consulted Ellen.

Her sister had passed the penny-bank stage and kept her money in a blue leather purse which was a proud possession. Aunt Elsie had given it to her last Christmas. It had two compartments and a small looking-glass—but there was very little money in it now. Ellen had already bought a good many presents. She was only able to change one quarter and one dime.

"Let's ask Derek," she said. "He loves to open his bank because he can use the screwdriver of his tool set."

Derek was delighted to show his savings—forty-five cents—but he was reluctant to give them all up for one quarter and two dimes. It would mean only three pieces to drop into the chimney of the little red house which was his bank.

"They don't clink at all," he complained, experimenting with the coins Sally held out. "You'll take all my money. I won't have hardly anything."

"You'll have *just* as much money to spend," explained Ellen.

"Yes," Derek admitted, "but not to jingle. I like the jingle. It sounds so much more."

He finally decided to change

one nickel and one dime.

Then Grandma changed a dime and Sally had sixty pennies all together to put into the pint cup. They brought the pile up about an inch.

When Father came home that night she asked him to change the fifty-cent piece, the quarter and the three nickels, but he did not have ninety cents in pennies and he said that he could not get them until Monday and now it was only Saturday.

"You understand, Sally," he explained looking down into his little daughter's anxious face, "you don't have any more money after this is changed. It only looks more."

"I know, but I want it that way," she answered. On Monday night he brought her the change and it made a full inch more of money in the cup. Still it was less than half a pint. Sally confided her discouragement to Ellen.

"Are you sure," asked her sister, "that it was this kind of present Mother wanted? She never asked for money before."

"I'm sure," Sally replied. "Uncle John said it was *cents* and that it would take a lot. Besides she prayed for it in church yesterday—so she must want it awfully."

"Prayed for it!" exclaimed Ellen in surprise.

"Yes. I heard her. It's that prayer we all say together. She asked God for 'two cents of all thy mercies.'"

"But if she wants a whole pint why did she only ask for 'two cents'?" demanded the practical Ellen.

"I don't know," sally answered. "Perhaps she thought it would be greedy. Mother is never greedy."

For several days things were at a standstill. Ellen caught a cold and passed it on to Sally and Derek. They were all put to bed and could do very little Christmas work. While Mother read aloud to them Sally finished her penwiper for Father and decorated a blotter for Uncle John—but sewing on Grandma's pincushion cover was difficult because the pillow at Sally's back kept slipping and she couldn't keep the needle straight. There seemed no way of adding anything to the pint cup.

"Mother, how could I earn some money quickly before Christmas?" Sally asked the first day that she was up.

"You have already earned a good deal, dear," Mother said. "Do you really need more?"

"Yes, Mother, lots more."

"How about getting 100 in your number work? Father gives you a

293

dime every time you do that."

"Yes," sighed Sally, "but it's very hard to get all the examples right. Don't you think when I get all right but one he might give me nine cents?"

"No," said Mother laughing. "Your father believes that nothing is good in arithmetic but 100."

She did earn one dime that way and then school closed, leaving no hope for anything more before Christmas.

On the twentieth of December there was a windfall. Aunt Elsie, who usually spent the holidays with them, was in the South and she sent Mother four dollars—one for each child for a Christmas present. "She told me to buy something for you," Mother explained, "but I thought perhaps you might like to spend the money yourselves—later on—during vacation."

"Oh! I'd like my dollar right away!" cried Sally delightedly. "And," she added rather shame-facedly, "Lovey is so little . . . do you think she needs all her money? Couldn't she give me half hers?"

"Why Sally, I'm surprised at you!" her mother answered. "I can't take your little sister's share for you. It wouldn't be fair. I am buying a new *Benjamin Bunny* for Lovey."

Aunt Elsie's gift brought the pennies in the pint cup a little above the half mark.

On the twenty-first Sally earned five cents by sweeping off the back porch. This had been a regular source of revenue in the fall, but when the dead leaves gave place to snow Mother forbade the sweeping. On the twenty-first there was no snow and Sally was allowed to go out with her little broom.

On the twenty-second Ellen and Sally went to a birthday party and Sally found a shiny bright dime in her piece of birthday cake. This helped a little. She and Ellen spent all their spare moments in shaking up the pennies in the pint measure—but they could not bring the level much above "One Half." Ellen was as excited over the plan now as Sally and she generously added her last four cents to the pile.

On the twenty-third Sally made a final desperate effort. "Mother," she said, "Uncle John is coming to dinner again tonight. Do you think he would be willing to give me my birthday dollar now?"

Mother smiled as she answered slowly—"But your birthday isn't till June. Isn't it rather strange to ask for your present so long ahead? Where is all this money going to?"

"It's a secret! My special secret!"

cried the little girl, taking her mother's reply for consent.

Uncle John gave her the dollar. She hugged and kissed him with delight and he said, "Let me always be your banker, Sally. I'm sorry you are so hard up, but don't take any wooden nickels."

"'Wooden nickels,'" she repeated slowly. "What are they? Perhaps they would fill up the bottom—"

"Of your purse?" Uncle John finished the sentence for her. "No, no, my dear. They are a very poor bottom for anything—and they are worse on top."

"It wasn't my purse," said Sally. "It was—but it's a secret."

When Father changed the birthday dollar into pennies he said,

"You are getting to be a regular little miser, my dear. I don't understand it. Where is all this money going to?"

"That's just what Mother asked," Sally answered. "It's a secret. You'll know on Christmas. Oh, Father, I think I have enough now!"

But she hadn't. The pennies seemed to melt away as they fell into the measure. She and Ellen took them all out three times and put them back again shaking them sideways and forwards, but it was no use. They looked a mountain on the nursery floor but they shrank in size the moment they were put inside that big cup. The mark stood obstinately below "Three Quarters."

"Oh! Ellen!" sobbed Sally after the third attempt. "Not even a pint! It's a horrid mean little present! All my presents are horrid. I never can give nice things like you! Oh dear, what shall I do!"

"Don't cry, Sally—please don't," said Ellen trying to comfort her little sister. "It's not a horrid present. It will look lovely when you put tissue paper around it and lots of red ribbon and a card. It *sounds* so much more than it looks," Ellen went on, giving the cup a vigorous jerk. "Why don't you print on your card 'Shake well before opening,' like our cough mixture?"

"I might," assented Sally, only partly reassured.

She had believed up to the last moment that she would be able to carry out her plan. It was vaguely associated in her mind with a miracle. Anything might happen at Christmas time but this year she had hoped for too much. It was so late now however that there was nothing to do but make the outside of her gift look as attractive as possible. She and Ellen spent most of the afternoon before Christmas wrapping up their presents. The pint cup was a little awkward in shape but they had it well covered and the red satin ribbon gathered tight at the top before Grandma made the final bow. It was a real rosette, for Sally had asked for something special.

Christmas Eve was almost more fun than Christmas. The Tuckers made a ceremony of hanging up their stockings. The whole family formed a line in the upper hall with Father at the head, the youngest child on his back, and then they marched downstairs keeping step to a Christmas chant. It was a home-made nonsense verse with a chorus of "Doodley-doodley, doodley-doo!" which everybody shouted. By the time they reached the living-room the line was in wild spirits.

The stockings were always hung in the same places. Father had the big armchair to the right of the fireplace and Mother the large mahogany chair opposite it, Lovey had a small white chair borrowed from the nursery. Derek tied his sock to the hook which usually held the fire tongs above the wood basket (it was a very inconvenient place but he liked it) and Ellen and Sally divided the sofa.

After the stockings were put up, one of the children recited the Bible verses, "And there were in the same country shepherds abiding in the field, keeping watch over their flock by night," through "Mary kept all these things and pondered them in her heart." Sally had said the

verses last Christmas—Ellen the
year before—and now it was
Derek's turn. He only forgot once
and Ellen prompted him softly.

Then they all sang Holy Night—
and Father read "'Twas the Night
Before Christmas." Last of all, the
children distributed their gifts for
the family—with a great many
stern directions: "Mother, you won't
look at this till tomorrow, will you?
Father, you promise not to peek?"
Then they went up to bed and by
morning Father and Mother and
Santa Claus had the stockings
stuffed full of things.

It went off as usual this year but
through all the singing and the
shouting Sally had twinges of
disappointment thinking of
Mother's unfinished present. She
had squeezed it into Mother's
stocking with some difficulty. Then
came Ellen's lovely towel and on

top of that Derek's calendar which
he had made in school.

There was a family rule at the
Tuckers' that stockings were not
opened until after breakfast.
Mother said that presents on an
empty stomach were bad for temper
and digestion and though it was
hard to swallow your cereal
Christmas morning,
the children knew
it was no use
protesting.

The first sight
of the living-room
was wonderful. The
place had completely changed over
night. Of course the stockings were
knobby with unknown delights, and
there were packages everywhere, on
the tables and chairs, and on the
floor big express boxes that had
come from distant places, marked
"Do Not Open Until Christmas."

Some presents are of such unmistakable shape that they cannot be hidden. Last year Derek had jumped right onto his rocking horse shouting, "It's mine! I know it's mine!" This morning he caught sight of a drum and looked no further. Lovey fell upon a white plush bunny. A lovely pink parasol was sticking out of the top of Sally's stocking and Ellen had a blue one. They just unfurled them over their heads and then watched Father and Mother unwrapping their presents.

The girls felt Derek and Lovey were very young because they emptied their stockings without a look towards the two big armchairs. That was the most thrilling moment, when your own offering came to view and Mother said, "Just what I wanted!" or Father, "How did you know I needed a penwiper?"

Mother always opened the children's presents first. She was untying the red ribbon on Ellen's towel now and reading the card which said "Every stitch a stitch of love." As she pulled off the tissue paper she exclaimed, "What beautiful work! What exquisite little stitches! Ellen—I am proud of you. This is a charming guest towel. Thank you, dear, so much."

"Grandma marked the cross-stitch for me," explained Ellen, "but I did all the rest myself."

Sally shivered with excitement as Mother's hand went down into her stocking again and tugged at the tin cup.

"Here is something very heavy," she said. "I can't guess what it is, and the card says 'Merry Christmas to Mother from Sally. Shake well before opening,' Is it medicine or cologne?"

299

Nobody remembered just what happened after that. Perhaps Grandma's bow was not tied tightly enough, perhaps Mother tilted the cup as she shook it, but in a moment all the pennies were on the floor. They rolled everywhere, past the chairs, into the grate, under the sofa and on to the remotest corners of the room. There was a terrific scramble. Father and Mother and Ellen and Sally and Derek, even Grandma and Lovey got down on their hands and knees to pick them up. They bumped elbows and knocked heads together and this onrush sent the coins flying everywhere. The harder they were chased the more perversely they hid themselves. Out of the hubbub Mother cried, "Sally dear, what is this? I don't understand. All your Christmas money for me? Darling, I can't take it."

Sally flung herself into her mother's arms with a sob. "Oh! you must!" she begged. "I'm sorry it's not a whole pint. I tried so hard. You said—you said—you wanted it most of all."

"Most of all?"

"Yes, judgment, cents. Uncle John said it was cents. You said even a pint would help. Won't half a pint be some good?"

Father and Mother and Grandma all laughed then. Father laughed almost as hard as Uncle John did when he first heard of Mother's list, and he declared that he was going to take Sally into the bank as a partner. But Mother lifted the little girl into her lap and whispered, "It's the most wonderful present I ever had. There's nothing so wonderful as sense—except love."

❄

Jingle Bells

1.

Dash-ing thru the snow, ___ in a one horse o - pen sleigh;

o'er the fields we go, laugh - ing all the way.

Bells on bob - tail ring, mak - ing spi - rits bright, what

Chorus

fun it is to ride and sing a sleigh-ing song to - night. Oh!

Jin - gle Bells, Jin - gle Bells! Jin - gle all the way!

Oh. what fun it is to ride in a

one horse o - pen sleigh. Oh, one horse o - pen sleigh!

2. Day or two ago
 I thought I'd take a ride,
 Soon Miss Fanny Bright
 Was seated at my side.
 The horse was lean and lank,
 Misfortune seem'd his lot,
 He got into a drifted bank,
 And we, we got upsot!

Chorus

3. Now the ground is white,
 Go it while you're young!
 Take the girls tonight,
 And sing this sleighing song.
 Just get a bobtail'd bay,
 Twoforty for his speed,
 Then hitch him to an open sleigh
 And crack! You'll take the lead.

Chorus

303

The Perfect Brownie Christmas Trees

*T*hese are absurdly easy and, perhaps, horribly commercial, but they are so sweet and so easy for kids to make. Leftover brownie pieces are wonderful crumbled over vanilla ice cream.

Your favorite brownie mix

Your favorite vanilla frosting

Green food coloring

Sprinkles, candy, or other decorations (such as M&M Mini Baking Bits)

1. Preheat oven to 350°F.

2. Line your 15 x 10 x 1-inch or 11 x 7 x 1-inch baking pan with foil. Butter and lightly flour the lining. Prepare a box of brownie mix according to package directions. Spread batter evenly in the greased pan.

3. Bake at 350°F for 20 minutes. Remove the pan from the oven and let cool completely. Lift out on the foil. Use a christmas tree cookie cutter to cut out tree shapes.

4. Add a few drops of green food coloring to your favorite packaged vanilla frosting. Frost and decorate.

About 15 brownies

Christmas Trees
A Christmas Circular Letter

Robert Frost

The city had withdrawn into itself
And left at last the country to the country;
When between whirls of snow not come to lie
And whirls of foliage not yet laid, there drove
A stranger to our yard, who looked the city,
Yet did in country fashion in that there
He sat and waited till he drew us out,
A-buttoning coats, to ask him who he was.
He proved to be the city come again
To look for something it had left behind
And could not do without and keep its Christmas.
He asked if I would sell my Christmas trees;

My woods—the young fir balsams like a place
Where houses all are churches and have spires.
I hadn't thought of them as Christmas trees.
I doubt if I was tempted for a moment
To sell them off their feet to go in cars
And leave the slope behind the house all bare,
Where the sun shines now no warmer than the moon.
I'd hate to have them know it if I was.
Yet more I'd hate to hold my trees, except
As others hold theirs or refuse for them,
Beyond the time of profitable growth—
The trial by market everything must come to.
I dallied so much with the thought of selling.
Then whether from mistaken courtesy
And fear of seeming short of speech, or whether
From hope of hearing good of what was mine,
I said, "There aren't enough to be worth while."

"I could soon tell how many they would cut,
You let me look them over."

                    "You could look.
But don't expect I'm going to let you have them."
Pasture they spring in, some in clumps too close
That lop each other of boughs, but not a few
Quite solitary and having equal boughs
All round and round. The latter he nodded "Yes" to,
Or paused to say beneath some lovelier one,
With a buyer's moderation, "That would do."
I thought so too, but wasn't there to say so.
We climbed the pasture on the south, crossed over,
And came down on the north.

                    He said, "A thousand."

"A thousand Christmas trees!—at what apiece?"

He felt some need of softening that to me:
"A thousand trees would come to thirty dollars."

Then I was certain I had never meant
To let him have them. Never show surprise!
But thirty dollars seemed so small beside
The extent of pasture I should strip, three cents
(For that was all they figured out apiece)—
Three cents so small beside the dollar friends
I should be writing to within the hour
Would pay in cities for good trees like those,
Regular vestry-trees whole Sunday Schools
Could hang enough on to pick off enough.

A thousand Christmas trees I didn't know I had!
Worth three cents more to give away than sell
As may be shown by a simple calculation.
Too bad I couldn't lay one in a letter.
I can't help wishing I could send you one,
In wishing you herewith a Merry Christmas.

The Gift of the Magi

O. Henry

One dollar and eighty-seven cents. That was all. And sixty cents of it was in pennies. Pennies saved one and two at a time by bulldozing the grocer and the vegetable man and the butcher until one's cheeks burned with the silent imputation of parsimony that such close dealing implied. Three times Della counted it. One dollar and eighty-seven cents. And the next day would be Christmas.

There was clearly nothing to do but flop down on the shabby little couch and howl. So Della did it. Which instigates the moral reflection that life is made up of sobs, sniffles, and smiles, with sniffles predominating.

While the mistress of the home is gradually subsiding from the first stage to the second, take a look at the home. A furnished flat at $8 per week. It did not exactly beggar description, but it certainly had that word on the lookout for the mendicancy squad.

In the vestibule below was a letter-box into which no letter would go, and an electric button from which no mortal finger could coax a ring. Also appertaining thereunto was a card bearing the name "Mr. James Dillingham Young."

The "Dillingham" had been flung to the breeze during a former period of prosperity when its possessor was being paid $30 per week. Now, when the income was shrunk to $20, the letters of "Dillingham" looked blurred, as though they were thinking seriously of contracting to a modest and unassuming D. But whenever Mr. James Dillingham Young came home and reached his flat above he was called "Jim" and greatly hugged by Mrs. James Dillingham Young, already introduced to you as Della. Which is all very good.

Della finished her cry and attended to her cheeks with the

powder rag. She stood by the window and looked out dully at a grey cat walking a grey fence in a grey backyard. To-morrow would be Christmas Day, and she had only $1.87 with which to buy Jim a present. She had been saving every penny she could for months, with this result. Twenty dollars a week doesn't go far. Expenses had been greater than she had calculated. They always are. Only $1.87 to buy a present for Jim. Her Jim. Many a happy hour she had spent planning for something nice for him. Something fine and rare and sterling—something just a little bit near to being worthy of the honour of being owned by Jim.

There was a pier-glass between the windows of the room. Perhaps you have seen a pier-glass in an $8 flat. A very thin and very agile person may, by observing his reflection in a rapid sequence of longitudinal strips, obtain a fairly accurate conception of his looks. Della, being slender, had mastered the art.

Suddenly she whirled from the window and stood before the glass. Her eyes were shining brilliantly, but her face had lost its colour within twenty seconds. Rapidly she pulled down her hair and let it fall to its full length.

Now, there were two possessions of the James Dillingham Youngs in which they both took a mighty pride. One was Jim's gold watch that had been his father's and grandfather's. The other was Della's hair. Had the Queen of Sheba lived in the flat across the airshaft, Della would have let her hair hang out the window some day to dry just to depreciate Her Majesty's jewels and gifts. Had King Solomon been the

janitor, with all his treasures piled up in the basement, Jim would have pulled out his watch every time he passed, just to see him pluck at his beard from envy.

So now Della's beautiful hair fell about her, rippling and shining like a cascade of brown waters. It reached below her knee and made itself almost a garment for her. And then she did it up again nervously and quickly. Once she faltered for a minute and stood still while a tear or two splashed on the worn red carpet.

On went her old brown jacket; on went her old brown hat. With a whirl of skirts and with the brilliant sparkle still in her eyes, she fluttered out the door and down

the stairs to the street.

Where she stopped the sign read: "Mme. Sofronie. Hair Goods of All Kinds." One flight up Della ran, and collected herself, panting. Madame, large, too white, chilly, hardly looked the "Sofronie."

"Will you buy my hair?" asked Della.

"I buy hair," said Madame. "Take yer hat off and let's have a sight at the looks of it."

Down rippled the brown cascade.

"Twenty dollars," said Madame, lifting the mass with a practised hand.

"Give it to me quick," said Della.

Oh, and the next two hours tripped by on rosy wings. Forget the hashed metaphor. She was ransacking the stores for Jim's present.

She found it at last. It surely had been made for Jim and no one else.

There was no other like it in any of the stores, and she had turned all of them inside out. It was a platinum fob chain simple and chaste in design, properly proclaiming its value by substance alone and not by meretricious ornamentation—as all good things should do. It was even worthy of The Watch. As soon as she saw it she knew that it must be Jim's. It was like him. Quietness and value—the description applied to both. Twenty-one dollars they took from her for it, and she hurried home with the 87 cents. With that chain on his watch Jim might be properly anxious about the time in any company. Grand as the watch was, he sometimes looked at it on the sly on account of the old leather strap that he used in place of a chain.

When Della reached home her intoxication gave way a little to prudence and reason. She got out her curling irons and lighted the gas and went to work repairing the ravages made by generosity added to love. Which is always a tremendous task, dear friends—a mammoth task.

Within forty minutes her head was covered with tiny close-lying curls that made her look wonderfully like a truant schoolboy. She looked at her reflection in the mirror long, carefully, and critically.

"If Jim doesn't kill me," she said to herself, "before he takes a second look at me, he'll say I look like a Coney Island chorus girl. But what could I do—oh! what could I do with a dollar and eighty-seven cents?"

At 7 o'clock the coffee was made and the frying-pan was on the back of the stove hot and ready to cook the chops.

Jim was never late. Della

doubled the fob chain in her hand and sat on the corner of the table near the door that he always entered. Then she heard his step on the stair away down on the first flight, and she turned white for just a moment. She had a habit of saying little silent prayers about the simplest everyday things, and now she whispered: "Please God, make him think I am still pretty."

The door opened and Jim stepped in and closed it. He looked thin and very serious. Poor fellow, he was only twenty-two—and to be burdened with a family! He needed a new overcoat and he was without gloves.

Jim stopped inside the door, as immovable as a setter at the scent

315

of quail. His eyes were fixed upon Della, and there was an expression in them that she could not read, and it terrified her. It was not anger, nor surprise, nor disapproval, nor horror, nor any of the sentiments that she had been prepared for. He simply stared at her fixedly with that peculiar expression on his face.

Della wriggled off the table and went for him.

"Jim, darling," she cried, "don't look at me that way. I had my hair cut off and sold it because I couldn't have lived through Christmas without giving you a present. It'll grow out again—you won't mind, will you? I just had to do it. My hair grows awfully fast. Say 'Merry Christmas!' Jim, and let's be happy. You don't know what a nice—what a beautiful, nice gift I've got for you."

"You've cut off your hair?" asked Jim, laboriously, as if he had not arrived at that patent fact yet even after the hardest mental labour.

"Cut it off and sold it," said Della. "Don't you like me just as well, anyhow? I'm me without my hair, ain't I?"

Jim looked about the room curiously.

"You say your hair is gone?" he said, with an air almost of idiocy.

"You needn't look for it," said Della. "It's sold, I tell you—sold and gone, too. It's Christmas Eve, boy. Be good to me, for it went for you. Maybe the hairs of my head were numbered," she went on with a sudden serious sweetness, "but nobody could ever count my love for you. Shall I put the chops on, Jim?"

Out of his trance Jim seemed

316

quickly to wake. He enfolded his Della. For ten seconds let us regard with discreet scrutiny some inconsequential object in the other direction. Eight dollars a week or a million a year—what is the difference? A mathematician or a wit would give you the wrong answer. The magi brought valuable gifts, but that was not among them. This dark assertion will be illuminated later on.

Jim drew a package from his overcoat pocket and threw it upon the table.

"Don't make any mistake, Dell," he said, "about me. I don't think there's anything in the way of a haircut or a shave or a shampoo that could make me like my girl any less. But if you'll unwrap that package you may see why you had me going a while at first."

White fingers and nimble tore at the string and paper. And then an ecstatic scream of joy; and then, alas! a quick feminine change to hysterical tears and wails, necessitating the immediate employment of all the comforting powers of the lord of the flat.

For there lay The Combs—the set of combs, side and back, that Della had worshipped for long in a Broadway window. Beautiful combs, pure tortoise shell, with jeweled rims—just the shade to wear in the beautiful vanished hair. They were expensive combs, she knew, and her heart had simply craved and yearned over them without the least hope of possession. And now, they were hers, but the tresses that should have adorned the coveted adornments were gone.

But she hugged them to her bosom, and at length she was able to look up with dim eyes and a smile and say: "My hair grows so fast, Jim!"

And then Della leaped up like a little singed cat and cried, "Oh, oh!"

Jim had not yet seen his beautiful present. She held it out to him eagerly upon her open palm. The dull precious metal seemed to flash with a reflection of her bright and ardent spirit.

"Isn't it a dandy, Jim? I hunted all over town to find it. You'll have to look at the time a hundred times a day now. Give me your watch. I want to see how it looks on it."

Instead of obeying, Jim tumbled down on the couch and put his hands under the back of his head and smiled.

"Dell," said he, "let's put our Christmas presents away and keep 'em a while. They're too nice to use just at present. I sold the watch to get the money to buy your combs. And now suppose you put the chops on."

The magi, as you know, were wise men—wonderfully wise men who brought gifts to the Babe in the manger. They invented the art of giving Christmas presents. Being wise, their gifts were no doubt wise ones, possibly bearing the privilege of exchange in case of duplication. And here I have lamely related to you the uneventful chronicle of two foolish children in a flat who most unwisely sacrificed for each other the greatest treasures of their house. But in a last word to the wise of these days let it be said that of all who give gifts these two were the wisest. Of all who give and receive gifts, such as they are wisest. Everywhere they are wisest. They are the magi.

❄

A Scandinavian Glögg

*T*he house will smell fabulous for days and the fruit compotes, which you will eat for days after Christmas, are spectacular.

1 quart port wine

1/4 pound raisins

1/4 pound whole blanched almonds

8 cardamom pods

5 whole cloves

3 cinnamon sticks

zest of lemon, cut into strips

zest of one naval orange,
    cut into strips

1/2 pound mixed dried apricots,
    apples, and prunes

1 quart dry red wine

aquavit

1. Pour port wine into nonaluminum saucepan with raisins and almonds. Put spices, zests, and dried fruits in strainer over pan so they are well covered by wine. (You may alter quantities to suit your taste.)

2. Simmer over low heat for 1 hour.

3. Turn off heat, cover, and let steep for one day.

4. To serve: remove strainer (you may wish to save fruits for delicious compote) and add dry red wine to the pot.

5. Heat mixture over low flame until very hot. Pour into glasses, add some raisins and almonds from pot, and add a tablespoon of aquavit.

Serves 8 to 14

My Christmas Miracle

Taylor Caldwell

For many of us, one Christmas stands out from all the others, the one when the meaning of the day shone clearest.

Although I did not guess it, my own "truest" Christmas began on a rainy spring day in the bleakest year of my life. Recently divorced, I was in my 20s, had no job, and was on my way downtown to go the rounds of the employment offices.

I had no umbrella, for my old one had fallen apart, and I could not afford another one. I sat down in the streetcar, and there against the seat was a beautiful silk umbrella with a silver handle inlaid with gold and flecks of bright enamel. I had never seen anything so lovely.

I examined the handle and saw a name engraved among the golden scrolls. The usual procedure would have been to turn in the umbrella to the conductor, but on impulse I decided to take it with me and find the owner myself. I got off the streetcar in a downpour and thankfully opened the umbrella to protect myself. Then I searched a telephone book for the name on the umbrella and found it. I called, and a lady answered.

Yes, she said in surprise, that was her umbrella, which her parents, now dead, had given her for a birthday present. But, she added, it had been stolen from her locker at school (she was a teacher) more than a year before. She was so excited that I forgot I was looking for a job and went directly to her small house. She took the umbrella, and her eyes filled with tears.

The teacher wanted to give me a reward, but—though $20 was all I had in the world—her happiness at retrieving this special possession was such that to have accepted money would have spoiled something. We talked for a while,

and I must have given her my address. I don't remember.

The next six months were wretched. I was able to obtain only temporary employment here and there, for a small salary, though this was what they now call the Roaring Twenties. But I put aside 25 or 50 cents when I could afford it for my little girl's Christmas presents. (It took me six months to save $8.) My last job ended the day before Christmas, my $30 rent was soon due, and I had $15 to my name— which Peggy and I would need for food. She was home from her convent boarding school and was excitedly looking forward to her gifts the next day, which I had already purchased. I had bought her a small tree, and we were going to decorate it that night.

The stormy air was full of the sound of Christmas merriment as I walked from the streetcar to my small apartment. Bells rang and children shouted in the bitter dusk of the evening, and windows were lighted and everyone was running and laughing. But there would be no Christmas for me, I knew, no gifts, no remembrance whatsoever. As I struggled through the snowdrifts, I just about reached the lowest point in my life. Unless a miracle happened I would be homeless in January, foodless, jobless. I had prayed steadily for weeks, and there had been no answer but this coldness and darkness, this harsh air, this abandonment. God and men had completely forgotten me. I felt old as death, and as lonely. What was to become of us?

I looked in my mailbox. There were only bills in it, a sheaf of them, and two white envelopes which I was sure contained more bills. I went up three dusty flights of stairs, and I cried, shivering in my thin coat. But I made myself smile so I could greet my little daughter with a pretense of happiness. She opened the door for me and threw herself in my arms, screaming joyously and demanding that we decorate the tree immediately.

Peggy was not yet six years old, and had been alone all day while I worked. She had set our kitchen table for our evening meal, proudly, and put pans out and the three cans of food which would be our dinner.

My Christmas Miracle

For some reason, when I looked at those pans and cans, I felt broken-hearted. We would have only hamburgers for our Christmas dinner tomorrow, and gelatin. I stood in the cold little kitchen, and misery overwhelmed me. For the first time in my life, I doubted the existence of God and His mercy, and the coldness in my heart was colder than ice.

The doorbell rang, and Peggy ran fleetly to answer it, calling that it must be Santa Claus. Then I heard a man talking heartily to her and went to the door. He was a delivery man, and his arms were full of big parcels, and he was laughing at my child's frenzied joy and her dancing. "This is a mistake," I said, but he read the name on the parcels, and they were for me. When he had gone I could only stare at the boxes. Peggy and I sat on the floor and opened them. A huge doll, three times the size of the one I had bought for her. Gloves. Candy. A beautiful leather purse. Incredible! I looked for the name of the sender. It was the teacher, the address simply "California," where she had moved.

Our dinner that night was the most delicious I had ever eaten. I could only pray in myself, "Thank You, Father." I forgot I had no money for the rent and only $15 in my purse and no job. My child and I ate and laughed together in happiness. Then we decorated the little tree and marveled at it. I put Peggy to bed and set up her gifts around the tree, and a sweet peace flooded me like a

benediction. I had some hope again. I could even examine the sheaf of bills without cringing. Then I opened the two white envelopes. One contained a check for $30 from a company I had worked for briefly in the summer. It was, said a note, my "Christmas bonus." My rent!

The other envelope was an offer of a permanent position with the government—to begin two days after Christmas. I sat with the letter in my hand and the check on the table before me, and I think that was the most joyful moment of my life up to that time.

The church bells began to ring. I hurriedly looked at my child, who was sleeping blissfully, and ran down to the street. Everywhere people were walking to church to celebrate the birth of the Saviour. People smiled at me and I smiled back. The storm had stopped, the sky was pure and glittering with stars.

"The Lord is born!" sang the bells to the crystal night and the laughing darkness. Someone began to sing, "Come, all ye faithful!" I joined in and sang with the strangers all about me.

I am not alone at all, I thought. *I was never alone at all.*

And that, of course, is the message of Christmas. We are never alone. Not when the night is darkest, the wind coldest, the world seemingly most indifferent. For this is still the time God chooses.

❄

329

God Rest You Merry, Gentlemen

1.

God Rest You Mer - ry, Gen - tle-men, let noth-ing you dis - may, Re -

mem-ber Christ our Sav - ior was born on Christ-mas day, To

Refrain

save us all from Sa -tan's pow'r, When we were gone a - stray. O, ___

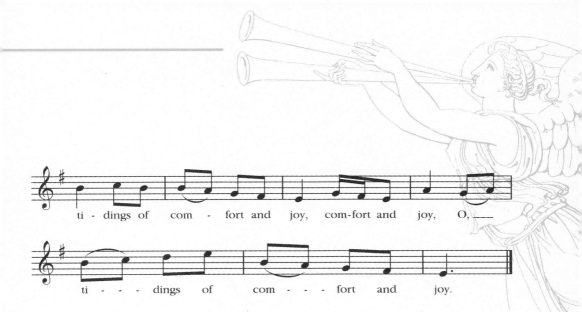

ti - dings of com - fort and joy, com-fort and joy, O,___ ti - - - dings of com - - - fort and joy.

2. "Fear not, then," said the angel,
Let nothing you affright,
This day is born a Saviour
Of a pure Virgin bright,
To free all those who trust in Him
From Satan's power and might."

Refrain

3. Now to the Lord sing praises,
All you within this place,
And with true love and brotherhood
Each other now embrace;
This holy tide of Christmas
All others doth deface.

Refrain

A Friend's Greeting

Edgar A. Guest

I'd like to be the sort of friend that you have been to me;
I'd like to be the help that you've been always glad to be;
I'd like to mean as much to you each minute of the day
As you have meant, old friend of mine, to me along the way.

I'd like to do the big things and the splendid things for you,
To brush the gray from out your skies and leave them only blue;
I'd like to say the kindly things that I so oft have heard,
And feel that I could rouse your soul the way that
    mine you've stirred.

I'd like to give you back the joy that you have given me,
Yet that were wishing you a need I hope will never be;
I'd like to make you feel as rich as I, who travel on
Undaunted in the darkest hours with you to lean upon.

I'm wishing at this Christmas time that I could but repay
A portion of the gladness that you've strewn along my way;
And could I have one wish this year, this only would it be:
I'd like to be the sort of friend that you have been to me.

A Gift
of the Heart

Norman Vincent Peale

New York city, where I live, is impressive at any time, but as Christmas approaches it's overwhelming. Store windows blaze with lights and color, furs and jewels. Golden angels, 40 feet tall, hover over Fifth Avenue. Wealth, power, opulence . . . nothing in the world can match this fabulous display.

Through the gleaming canyons, people hurry to find last-minute gifts. Money seems to be no problem. If there's a problem, it's that the recipients so often have everything they need or want that it's hard to find anything suitable, anything that will really say, "I love you."

Last December, as Christ's birthday drew near, a stranger was faced with just that problem. She had come from Switzerland to live in an American home and perfect her English. In return, she was willing to act as secretary, mind the grandchildren, do anything she was asked. She was just a girl in her late teens. Her name was Ursula.

One of the tasks her employers gave Ursula was keeping track of Christmas presents as they arrived. There were many, and all would require acknowledgment. Ursula kept a faithful record, but with a

A Gift of the Heart

growing sense of concern. She was grateful to her American friends; she wanted to show her gratitude by giving them a Christmas present. But nothing that she could buy with her small allowance could compare with the gifts she was recording daily. Besides, even without these gifts, it seemed to her that her employers already had everything.

At night from her window Ursula could see the snowy expanse of Central Park and beyond it the jagged skyline of the city. Far below, taxis hooted and the traffic lights winked red and green. It was so different from the silent majesty of the Alps that at times she had to blink back tears of the homesickness she was careful never to show. It was in the solitude of her little room, a few days before Christmas, that her secret idea came to Ursula.

It was almost as if a voice spoke clearly, inside her head. "It's true," said the voice, "that many people in this city have much more than you do. but surely there are many who have far less. If you will think about this, you may find a solution to what's troubling you."

Ursula thought long and hard. Finally, on her day off, which was Christmas Eve, she went to a large department store. She moved slowly along the crowded aisles, selecting and rejecting things in her mind. At last she bought something and had it wrapped in gaily colored paper. She went out into the gray twilight and looked helplessly around. Finally, she went up to a doorman, resplendent in blue and gold. "Excuse, please," she said in her hesitant English, "can you tell me where to find a poor street?"

"A poor street, Miss?" said the puzzled man.

"Yes, a very poor street. The poorest in the city."

The doorman looked doubtful. "Well, you might try Harlem. Or down in the Village. Or the Lower East Side, maybe."

But these names meant nothing to Ursula. She thanked the doorman and walked along, threading her way through the stream of shoppers until she came to a tall policeman. "Please," she said, "can you direct me to a very poor street in . . . in Harlem?"

The policeman looked at her sharply and shook his head.

"Harlem's no place for you, Miss." And he blew his whistle and sent the traffic swirling past.

Holding her package carefully, Ursula walked on, head bowed against the sharp wind. If a street looked poorer than the one she was on, she took it. But none seemed like the slums she had heard about. Once she stopped a woman, "Please, where do the very poor people live?" But the woman gave her a stare and hurried on.

Darkness came sifting from the sky. Ursula was cold and discouraged and afraid of becoming lost. She came to an intersection and stood forlornly on the corner. What she was trying to do suddenly seemed foolish, impulsive, absurd. Then, through the traffic's roar, she heard the cheerful tinkle of a bell. On the corner opposite, a Salvation Army man was making his traditional Christmas appeal.

At once Ursula felt better; the Salvation Army was a part of life in Switzerland too. Surely this man could tell her what she wanted to know. She waited for the light, then crossed over to him. "Can you help me? I'm looking for a baby. I have here a little present for the poorest baby I can find." And she held up the package with the green ribbon and the gaily colored paper.

Dressed in gloves and overcoat a size too big for him, he seemed a very ordinary man. But behind his steel-rimmed glasses his eyes were kind. He looked at Ursula and stopped ringing his bell. "What sort of present?" he asked.

"A little dress. For a small, poor baby. Do you know of one?"

"Oh, yes," he said. "Of more than one, I'm afraid."

"Is it far away? I could take a taxi, maybe?"

The Salvation Army man wrinkled his forehead. Finally he said, "It's almost six o'clock. My relief will show up then. If you want to wait, and if you can afford a dollar taxi ride, I'll take you to a family in my own neighborhood who needs just about everything."

"And they have a small baby?"

"A very small baby."

"Then," said Ursula joyfully, "I wait!"

The substitute bell-ringer came. A cruising taxi slowed. In its welcome warmth, Ursula told her new friend about herself, how she came to be in New York, what she was trying to do. He listened in silence, and the taxi driver listened too. When they reached their destination, the driver said, "Take your time, Miss. I'll wait for you."

On the sidewalk, Ursula stared up at the forbidding tenement, dark, decaying, saturated with hopelessness. A gust of wind, iron-cold, stirred the refuse in the street and rattled the ashcans. "They live on the third floor," the Salvation Army man said. "Shall we go up?"

But Ursula shook her head. "They would try to thank me, and this is not from me." She pressed the package into his hand. "Take it up for me, please. Say it's from . . . from someone who has everything."

The taxi bore her swiftly back from dark streets to lighted ones, from misery to abundance. She tried to visualize the Salvation Army man climbing the stairs, the knock, the explanation, the package being opened, the dress on the baby. It was hard to do.

Arriving at the apartment house on Fifth Avenue where she lived, she fumbled in her purse. But the driver flicked the flag up. "No charge, Miss."

"No charge?" echoed Ursula, bewildered.

A Gift of the Heart

"Don't worry," the driver said. "I've been paid." He smiled at her and drove away.

Ursula was up early the next day. She set the table with special care. By the time she had finished, the family was awake, and there was all the excitement and laughter of Christmas morning. Soon the living room was a sea of gay discarded wrappings. Ursula thanked everyone for the presents she received. Finally, when there was a lull, she began to explain hesitantly why there seemed to be none from her. She told about going to the department store. She told about the Salvation Army man. She told about the taxi driver. When she finished, there was a long silence. No one seemed to trust himself to speak. "So you see," said Ursula, "I try to do a kindness in your name. And this is my Christmas present to you. . . ."

How do I happen to know all this? I know it because ours was the home where Ursula lived. Ours was the Christmas she shared. We were like many Americans, so richly blessed that to this child from across the sea there seemed to be nothing she could add to the material things we already had. And so she offered something of far greater value: a gift of the heart, an act of kindness carried out in our name.

Strange, isn't it? A shy Swiss girl, alone in a great impersonal city. You would think that nothing she could do would affect anyone. And yet, by trying to give away love, she brought the true spirit of Christmas into our lives, the spirit of selfless giving. That was Ursula's secret— and she shared it with us all.

❄

343

Well, so that is that

W. H. Auden

Well, so that is that. Now we must dismantle the tree,
Putting the decorations back into their cardboard boxes—
Some have got broken—and carrying them up to the attic.
The holly and mistletoe must be taken down and burnt,
And the children got ready for school. There are enough
Left-overs to do, warmed up, for the rest of the week—
Not that we have much appetite, having drunk such a lot,
Stayed up so late, attempted—quite unsuccessfully—
To love all our relatives, and in general
Grossly overestimated our powers. Once again
As in previous years we have seen the actual Vision and failed
To do more than entertain it as an agreeable
Possibility, once again we have sent Him away
Begging though to remain His disobedient servant,
The promising child who cannot keep His word for long.

Silent Night

1.

Si - lent Night, ho - - - ly night,

all is calm, all is bright.

'Round yon vir - gin moth - er and child.

Ho - ly in - fant so ten - der and mild,

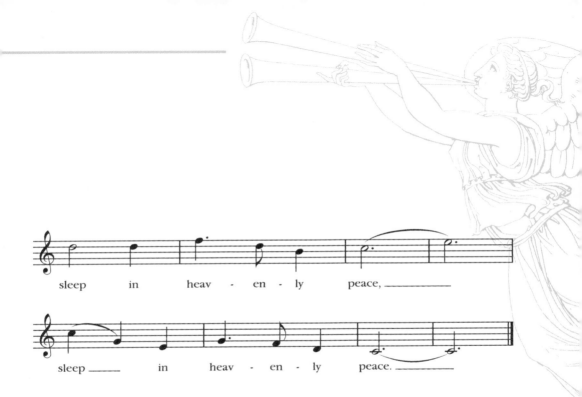

sleep in heav - en - ly peace, _____

sleep _____ in heav - en - ly peace. _____

2. Silent night! Holy night!
Shepherds quake at the sight!
Glories stream from Heaven afar,
Heav'nly hosts sing Alleluia,
Christ, the Saviour, is born!
Christ, the Saviour, is born!

3. Silent night! Holy night!
Son of God, love's pure light,
Radiant beams from Thy holy face,
With the dawn of redeeming grace,
Jesus, Lord, at Thy birth,
Jesus, Lord, at Thy birth.

Helpful Cookie Hints

* Have lots of cookie trays, parchment paper (if possible), rolling pins, cookie cutters, airtight containers (collect cookie tins for this occasion), and decorations bought well ahead. There is nothing more disappointing than going to your local supermarket a week before Christmas and finding the shelves bare! You can order decorations, including gold and silver "luster dust," from New York Cake & Baking Distributors at (212) 675-2253 or other baking suppliers, and cookie cutters can be found in antique stores, as well as kitchen supply stores.

* If the dough becomes too soft to work, roll it up in some waxed paper and put it back in the refrigerator for a 1/2 hour.

* If you don't use all the dough, wrap it up and return it to the refrigerator for up to a week or the freezer for up to 3 months.

* Use a plastic drinking straw or skewer to make holes in cookies where you want to run a ribbon or string through to turn them into ornaments or gift tags. For this purpose you can make cookies thicker than usual, in which case you should bake them longer at a lower temperature (approximately 25 to 30 minutes at 325°F).

* If you are rolling dough between two sheets of waxed or parchment paper, sprinkle your work surface with a bit of water to prevent the paper from sliding.

* Butter cookie sheets or line them with parchment paper. If you use nonstick cookie sheets, the cookies will brown a bit faster.

* If possible, use cookie sheets with 3 open sides, or at least one open side, so you can slide the parchment sheet off with the cookies.

* Try to use sheets that have a 2" space on each side in the oven, so the heat can circulate.

* Cool sheets between taking

them out of the oven and refilling them with cookies.

* Do not put cookies away until they are completely cool.

* Wash all nonplastic cookie cutters in warm soapy water and dry them immediately to keep them from rusting. Cookie sheets can dry in a turned-off but warm oven.

Helpful Icing Hints

* You can decorate with sugar crystals, silver balls, or nonpareils before cookies go into the oven BUT don't ice until cookies have cooled.

* Add food coloring slowly to be sure you get the shade you want.

* When not working with the icing, keep it covered with plastic wrap so it doesn't dry out. If you don't use it all, you can keep it covered in the refrigerator for up to 2 weeks.

* Keep icing thin for coating cookies with a brush. Keep icing thick for piping.

(Icing can be thinned with egg whites.)

* To pipe icing: Fill the decorating bag by setting it in a tall glass or jar. Fold the top of the bag over the rim and spoon frosting into the bag. If you use a disposable bag, cut the tip off and fit a piping tip in before adding the frosting. If you use a ziplock bag, put frosting in, squeeze all air from the bag, seal, and snip off the tip of one corner.

* Pipe an outline first to keep thinned icing from flowing off the cookie. Let piping dry for 5 minutes before coating. Coat and let dry. Now paint or pipe icing where you want the decoration to stick. Or, try using a sponge dipped into a color, apply to a cookie coated with white, and you'll have "spatterware"!

* Toothpicks are great for mixing colors into the icing, and for dipping into the icing and drawing.

Acknowledgments

"Well so that is that..." from "The Flight Into Egypt" from *W.H. Auden: Collected Poems* by W.H. Auden, edited by Edward Mendelson. Copyright © 1944 and renewed 1972 by W.H. Auden. Reprinted by permission of Random House, Inc.

"The Three Magi" by Pura Belpré. Copyright © 1977 Pura Belpré, Eliseo Torres; first appeared in *The Animals' Christmas* by Anne Eaton published by The Viking Press.

"My Christmas Miracle" by Taylor Caldwell. Reprinted by permission of *Family Weekly*, copyright © 1968, 641 Lexington Avenue , New York, New York 10022.

"Mistletoe" by Walter de la Mare. Reprinted with permission of The Literary Trustees of Walter de la Mare, and the Society of Authors as their representative.

"Our Lady's Juggler" by Anatole France. From *Mother of Pearl*, a translation by Frederic Chapman, Books for Libraries, 1970. Reprinted by permission of Ayer Company Publishers.

"Christmas Trees: A Christmas Circular Letter" from "Christmas Trees" from *The Poetry of Robert Frost*, edited by Edward Connery Lathem. Copyright 1916, copyright 1944 by Robert Frost. © 1969 by Henry Holt and Company, Inc. Reprinted by permission of Henry Holt and Company, Inc.

"The Miraculous Staircase" by Arthur Gordon. Reprinted with permission from Guideposts Magazine. Copyright © 1966, 1981 by Guideposts, Carmel, New York 10512.

"Carol of the Field Mice" from *The Wind in the Willows* by Kenneth Grahame. Copyright The University Chest, Oxford, reproduced by permission of Curtis Brown Ltd., London.

"Silent Night" by Franz Gruber.

"Joy to the World" by George F. Handel.

"We Three Kings of Orient Are" by J. H. Hopkins, Jr.

"Christmas Eve at Sea" by John Masefield. Reprinted with permission of The Society of Authors as the literary representative of the Estate of John Masefield.

"Hark! The Herald Angels Sing" by Felix Mendelssohn and Charles Wesley.

"A Carol for Children" from *Verses from 1929 and On* by Ogden Nash. Copyright 1934 by Ogden Nash; first appeared in The New Yorker. By permission of Little, Brown and Company.

"A Gift of the Heart" by Norman Vincent Peale. Reprinted with permission from the January 1968 Reader's Digest. Copyright © 1968 by The Reader's Digest Assn., Inc.

"Jingel Bells" by James Pierpont.

"O Little Town of Bethlehem" by L. H. Redner.

Illustration on page 10 by Jessie Wilcox Smith.

"A Miserable, Merry Christmas" from *The Autobiography of Lincoln Steffens*, by Lincoln Steffens. Copyright 1931 by Harcourt, Inc. and renewed 1959 by Peter Steffens, reprinted by permission of the publisher.

"Christmas This Year" by Booth Tarkington. Privately printed by Booth Tarkington, 1945. Permission granted by Estate of Booth Tarkington.

"Once on Christmas" by Dorothy Thompson. Copyright 1938 by Oxford University Press. Renewed 1966 by Michael Lewis.

Illustration on page 236-237 by Ida Waugh.

Every attempt has been made to obtain permission to reproduce materials protected by copyright. Where omissions may have occurred, the producers will be happy to acknowledge this in future printings.